KOBE BRY
BIOGRAPHY

"I'll do whatever it takes to win games, whether it's sitting on a bench waving a towel, handing a cup of water to a teammate, or hitting the game-winning shot."

Kevin Gregory Brannan

-BIOGRAPHY-

KOBE BRYANT

Legendary Journey of Black Mamba

CONTENTS

INTRODUCTION

An inside look at one of our culture's most compelling and influential personalities, using never-before-heard interviews. Kobe Bryant's death in January 2020 did more than shake the sports and celebrity worlds. The tragedy of that helicopter crash, which also killed his daughter Gianna, revealed the full breadth and depth of his influence on our culture, and the book promises to provide an insight into Kobe that no other analysis has by tracing and telling the oft-forgotten and lesser-known story of his early life.

Listeners will travel from the Southwest Philadelphia neighbourhood streets, where Kobe's father, Joe, was a local basketball standout, to the Bryant family's isolation in Italy, where Kobe spent his formative years, to the leafy suburbs of Lower Merion, where Kobe's legend was born. The film will follow Kobe's life and career at Lower Merion, where he led the Aces to the 1995-96 Pennsylvania state championship, a dramatic underdog run for a team with only one star player, and the lead-up to the 1996 NBA draft, where he was selected by the Los Angeles Lakers. Mike Sielski had a huge edge over other writers who have attempted to document Kobe's life when researching and writing the book: access to a series of never-before-released interviews with him throughout his senior season and early days in the NBA. These tapes and transcripts preserved Kobe's youthful ideas, dreams, and goals, and they included insights into and conveyed stories about him that had never been revealed before. This isn't just another basketball audiobook. This is an investigation into the identity and formation of an icon, as well as the impact of his growth on others around him - the essence of the man before he truly became a man.

St. Martin's Press's Macmillan Audio production

CHAPTER 1

OK, LET'S PLAY

Peers from Kobe Bryant's past don't remember him as a Los Angeles Laker, a five-time NBA champion, or a nonpareil of competitive nature who bestowed upon himself an outrageous nickname—Mamba—that he turned into an eponymous lifestyle brand. This was the time Evan Monsky was driving home one night over the phone. That was not their Kobe. Kobe? Monsky wasn't sure what that Kobe had in common with their Kobe. "From the time he was eighteen until his dying day, people kissed this dude's ass," he explained, "and it's a crazy type of ass-kissing." It's not a normal life, and it's not one that many people would cherish. It appears to be a heinous crime." And what did that life do to Kobe? What effect did it have on him? Those who knew him when he was younger had a particular memory of him. Was he still that person?

There's a part of Monsky, and probably everyone who met Kobe at Lower Merion, who doesn't want the answers to those questions. Monsky remembered a kid, a sixteen-year-old kid, who loved to talk hoops, who wasn't the funniest guy in the room but could crack a decent joke now and then, who got nervous whenever the vehicle he was travelling in, whether his car, his parents' car, or a school bus full of basketball players, had to cross a bridge. Monsky doesn't value those memories because they are uncommon. They're valuable to him because they aren't, because they're recollections of a sixteen-year-old boy, not the world's most famous athlete. They're recollections of a kid who shared a seat with him on afternoon rides to games and evening rides from games, who would look out the window and whose lungs would swell and compress in horror at the silvery lake below. There was no explanation for Kobe's terror in those few seconds, at least none that he would disclose to his teammates. But they'd ridicule him about it like if he were one of them, which in their minds he was and always would be, and he'd white-knuckle it until the bus arrived safely on the other side.

Perhaps as he allowed himself to imagine winning a district or perhaps a state title at the start of Kobe's junior year, Gregg Downer realised that if the Aces were to achieve such heights, he needed to make some changes, and his finest player needed reinforcements. Some of those changes and reinforcements would emerge naturally as a result of Kobe's growth and the return of numerous key players for the 1994-95 school year and basketball season. Lower Merion's 16-6 record, and even its district-playoff loss to Plymouth Whitemarsh, a strong team that qualified for the state championship tournament, had reaffirmed to Downer and the upperclassmen that the Aces could, and probably should, be among the best teams in the Philadelphia area and all of Pennsylvania. Downer frequently encouraged his players to aim for the District One semi finals since those two games were hosted yearly at the Palestra, and playing at the Palestra meant experiencing and achieving something exceptional. But he also knew that the squad was missing some critical components, both material and intangible, that it needed not only to get that far in the postseason, but also to win once there.

Dan Pangrazio transferred in for his freshman year when his family relocated to the Main Line in the fall of 1994, and he was one such component. Pangrazio was a preteen athletic superstar in his birthplace of Fairfield, Connecticut. He was nine when he won the Connecticut and New England titles in the Elks Hoop Shoot, a free-throw-shooting contest sponsored nationally by the Benevolent and Protective Order of Elks—an accomplishment that earned him a 671-word story in The New York Times on April 9, 1989. Pangrazio would be the Aces' starting shooting guard, balancing the offence's alignment and requiring opponents to respect his ability to make a long jumper, or several. As much as Kobe's presence was a boon, Downer and the Aces couldn't rely on him too much. What if he got into mischief? What if he becomes injured? Downer used to make people laugh by saying, "I'm one Kobe Bryant sprained ankle away from being a total schmuck."

The offensive boost that Pangrazio would almost certainly offer would be great, but Downer's more pressing goal was to improve the

Aces' defence. They had given up an average of seventy points in their final eight games of the '93-'94 season, putting too much pressure on Kobe and his teammates to go basket for hoop against teams with higher overall skill. Downer had met Mike Egan, an Ardmore native who had just finished his second season as an assistant coach at Wilmington College, an NAIA college in New Castle, Delaware, through the Narberth League. Living in the Overbrook neighbourhood of Philadelphia, working as an insurance underwriter in southern New Jersey, and coaching in northern Delaware made for an arduous schedule, especially for a twenty-nine-year-old man like Egan, who was unmarried and had few attachments and duties. Coaching at Lower Merion would allow him to work with Kobe and reduce the amount of time he spent in his car; Egan had seen him play in Narberth summer ball and had played pickup against him at the Jewish Community Center. "I was like, 'This kid is worth going back to the high school ranks to coach,'" he explained, and Downer made him an appealing offer: "Be my defensive coordinator." No basketball team has ever won a championship without excellent half-court defence. Every night, I'll give you twenty minutes to conduct practice and coach your system your way. Egan was powerless to refuse.

The third and last item on Downer's list was possibly the most important and meaningful. If the Aces were to compete with, let alone beat, the finest competition in the region and state, they needed to get used to facing such teams before the tournament. So Downer began to beef up their non conference schedule. They would play their sixteen annual Central League games, but Downer would fill up any open dates with a higher rated opponent: St. Anthony in Jersey City, led by Bob Hurley, Bobby Hurley's father and one of only three high school coaches inducted into the Naismith Memorial Basketball Hall of Fame; Glen Mills, a Delaware County youth detention centre whose high school basketball team competed against public and private high schools throughout Pennsylvania; and Coatesville, with a blade-thin junior sharpening himself into one of the area's best guards: Richard "Rip" Hamilto. Downer had spent three days in Harrisburg the previous summer coaching a Philadelphia-area all-star squad at the Keystone Games, Pennsylvania's equivalent of the

Olympics. The guys he coached there came from the city's annual blue-chip boys' basketball schools, as well as one located not within Philadelphia, but just outside of it: the Chester High School Clippers, the class of District One, and the defending state champions. These teams were identical to those that Downer had added to Lower Merion's expanded schedule. He wanted to expose his team to those kids' toughness and grit. Kobe had it, but the others needed to feel it, touch it. Chester, in particular, exemplified that edge, toughness, and excellence; in 1994, it won its third state championship in twelve years. Downer and Kobe were already keeping an eye on the Clippers, since the two of them saw Chester as the benchmark they aimed for, as the greatest threat to their success.

Anthony Gilbert's connection with Kobe Bryant arose from his delicate flirtation with Sharia Bryant. She was a standout on Temple University's women's volleyball team, an outside hitter with that Bryant family leaping ability, thwacking one kill after another until she finished fifth on the Owls' all-time list, five foot ten with striking features but so approachable and down-to-earth off the court. He was a part-time freshman at Temple who was working in the athletic department to make his way through school and didn't know the first thing about volleyball when he began handling statistics and research for the team. He was five feet eight, so he not only looked up to Sharia, but also at Sharia. He was impressed by her and wanted to impress her more.

As Kobe's junior season began, the coaching staff indicated his importance to the Aces by selecting him team captain. I am not a team captain. The captain of the team. Not all of his teammates accepted the decision with grace and understanding. Monsky had assumed that as seniors, he and Guy Stewart—the former outspoken, the later a follow-by-example type—would split leadership duties, and he was disappointed that the coaches had passed them over for Kobe. It was the first of several instances of tension and arrogance in the early stages of the season. In an interview with Stacy Moscotti, a writer for The Merionite, Kobe boasted that the Aces had a very good chance of winning the state championship. "I look around at those other teams," he continued, "and they're not even close to as good as we are." Egan scribbled his impressions of each player in black felt-tip pen on loose-leaf paper during his first few practices with the team, and his evaluations of Kobe revealed the new assistant coach to be an unforgiving grader: "offensive, foul prone; lateral movement; work on rebounding, shot selection... Playing poorly, must rebound more, dominate from 15 feet or more in plus then 3 will come. You are only as excellent as your level of commitment. Don't be careless." Then, as karmic retribution for Kobe's comments to The Merionite, the Aces opened their season with a 62-60 loss to Sun Valley, a game in which they blew a fourth-quarter lead and Kobe, with 31 points, and Dan Pangrazio, with sixteen, combined for 78 percent of the offence. That distribution suggested that the club was still too top-heavy, that the same dilemma that had hung over Downers head like an anvil for two years—when is there too much Kobe, and when is there too little?—remained unsolved. Downer and Egan approached Kobe before the team's second game, its first Central League game of the season, against Upper Darby, and urged him to be more outspoken with his teammates, to include them more. Kobe promised to demonstrate his leadership through his play.

Over the next two months, what he showed them was breathtaking. He scored more than thirty points each game in the Aces' next three games, all of which they won by at least fourteen points. He went into his next game, against Marple Newtown, five days before Christmas knowing he had 994 career points, six short of 1,000, and after hitting his first two shots, he tightened up, missing his next three and committing a turnover, his anxiety over reaching the milestone causing him to press. Finally, with three and a half minutes remaining in the first quarter, he splashed a jump shot from near the foul line. Lower Merion triumphed, 63-58. He had 38 points, a career high, which he then surpassed two nights later, scoring forty in a thirteen-point win against Penncrest that was notable for something else, something darker: The game included the first documented and sustained public criticism of and pushback against Kobe Bryant in his life, and to call what happened "criticism" is an understatement.

The NCAA established Proposition 48 in 1986, which said that a high school student who wanted to play Division I sports in college had to achieve specific academic standards, including grades and SAT scores. For example, the minimum SAT requirement was 700 points, whereas a perfect score was 1600. "A Prop 48 kid" quickly became racist, stereotypical shorthand for insulting a basketball player, almost typically a Black basketball player, by describing him or her as foolish enough to be admitted to college. Once the referee sent the ball up for the first tip-off, a section of Penncrest fans, white Penncrest fans, began hurling racial epithets and yelling at Kobe: "PROP 48! PROP 48!"

But that was merely the beginning. Kobe's prominence was rising, as were the stakes for everyone involved, including the Bryants. Kobe's games had become such a priority for the family that Shaya, the starting centre for the girls' basketball team, had skipped a handful of her own games to attend Kobe's. "Of course, we'd lose," Tolbert, one of Shaya's teammates, claimed, "because she was the one everyone feared, and I was only five ten." The machine that surrounded him was extraordinarily close-knit." Tales of Kobe's talent were now spreading across Philadelphia and its environs, thanks to locker-room talk, coaches' meetings, and college scouts' insight swaps, with so much of the conversation organic. Jeremy Treatman, who was still stringing for The Inquirer, still talking with Joe on a regular basis and checking in with Kobe once a week, and still visiting Lower Merion's practices and games, couldn't persuade his editors that Kobe deserved a major profile piece or even increased attention, but he soon had an alternative medium available to him: Kobe's own website. He started as a producer and on-air reporter for The Inquirer High School Sports Show, a weekly TV show sponsored by the paper that featured local players. When the district playoffs arrived and attention began to grow, he could relate Kobe's story there. To stay up to date on Kobe, you had to be on the ground, attending games or reading the local newspapers and weeklies on the Main Line and in Delaware County. Regardless, the word was getting out. They must be followed.' All of the

The Aces' winning streak had reached eight games ahead of their first of two games against Ridley, whose coach, John DiGregorio, had given Kobe yet another boost of incentive. Those Central League triumphs, as satisfying as they were, were never going to be the best barometer of Kobe's and the Aces' position in the state. Those non-league games, which Downer had planned, had been on the coaching staff's collective mind since the preseason, influencing Egan's defensive scheme and stretching Kobe's patience and stubbornness to their limits. Egan's method called for the guards and forwards to pressure the ball and draw the dribbler into a double-team or trap, and also required Kobe, who played in the post, to always front his man.

Now came the chance for the 11-1 Aces to put their preparation to the test: a late Saturday afternoon away game against Rip Hamilton and a 12-3 Coatesville team. Nothing about the environment was relaxing or soothing to them. In comparison to their more intimate environment, the gym felt like the Louisiana Superdome. It had a scoreboard that displayed the numbers of the players on the floor and kept track of their points and fouls, which was a mind-blowing sight for the Aces. The teams had never played each other before. They were set to play the previous season, but the game was cancelled due to an ice storm, thus Hamilton remained as mythological and unknown to most of Kobe's coaches and teammates as Kobe remained to Hamilton's. Downer warned the Aces that the Coatesville standout, who was smart and had a quicksilver style, penetrating and setting up teammates one minute and shredding defences the next, would be the best player they would face all season. Similarly, when someone informed Hamilton that there was a guard at Lower Merion his age, size, with superior shooting range and more jazz to his game, who could do everything Hamilton could and a few things he couldn't, it seemed nonsensical. Outside of Coatesville, Hamilton had hardly played basketball. He hadn't been trained and spoiled like Kobe—he'd turned up to his first high school basketball trial wearing platform shoes without heels—and he'd struggled to accept the fact that, in comparison to everyone else, he was the lesser player. Lower Merion, perhaps? There are no youngsters from the neighbourhood where I grew up, Hamilton reasoned. It's similar to a private school. He's still not up to par with me. He is still unable to outperform me.

"You hear so much about a kid who's good," Coatesville assistant coach Rick Hicks said, "and you think you've got one of the best players in the area." 'Somebody's better than him?' you ponder. I had to visit him.' It was all Kobe's swag, and I'm not talking about arrogant swag. 'I'm telling you I'm going to steal the ball, and I'll steal it,' he said. 'I say I'm going to do this, and I do it.'"

That afternoon, Kobe's performance reflected that ethos. The Red Raiders used a box-and-one defence against him, and Downer informed the rest of the squad during a timeout, "You guys are going to have to make open shots for us to win." Stewart, Pangrazio, and Jermaine Griffin did; the trio combined for 43 points, with each scoring in double figures, and Lower Merion led by two with less than ten seconds remaining in regulation. But Hamilton, on the right wing, performed a balletic spin move, dipped under Kobe, and sank a layup with five seconds remaining, sending the game into overtime. He fouled out with 75 seconds left in the extra period, ending with 21 points, but Coatesville maintained a four-point advantage following his exit. A four-point deficit in the last minute of a game is far from insurmountable in the NBA, and even in college basketball. A four-point deficit in the last minute of a high school basketball game indicated the Aces were pretty much toast. Almost anything.

Jim "Scoogie" Smith could see it all clearly in his mind's eye twenty-five years later, and it still gave him a twinge of sadness and appreciation. Smith was an assistant coach for Coatesville that day, like Hicks, and he was on his feet as a Lower Merion player brought down a defensive rebound and hit Kobe in stride with an outlet ball. Kobe sprinted to his right toward the sideline and crossed half-court after four dribbles. "What was so amazing about him," Smith added, "was that once he got over half-court, he didn't do what most players do." He didn't fire a shot with just one hand. He took another one and a half, maybe two dribbles, and hit a jump shot."

When Kobe rose to shoot, he was twenty-five feet from the rim, directly in front of Smith and Hicks and the Coatesville bench. Hicks thought to himself, "There's no way in hell that shot is going in."

The shot was successful.

It had now become a one-point game. To halt the clock, the Aces committed a foul. A Red Raiders player failed to convert the first half of a one-and-one. Kobe grabbed the rebound and sent the ball up court toward the right sideline once more. He cut to his left this time, evading a defender near the free-throw line, and slid into the lane, pulling up for a six-foot jumper. With two seconds remaining, the ball slipped through the netting of the basket like a feather. Coatesville 77, Lower Merion 78. Later that night, at home, Hamilton replayed the game in his thoughts, comparing himself to Kobe and feeling unsatisfied. You're not who you thought you were, bro.

"That might have been the best basketball game we played in all of Kobe's years," Egan remarked.

The Aces showered, changed, and carried their duffel bags out to the court to greet their family members who were socialising. Shaya Bryant gazed up at Coatesville's massive scoreboard, which was still flashing with the players' final statistics, after Monsky had gone the entire game without scoring. There was a 0 next to Monsky's jersey number, No. 31. A 32 was next to Kobe's No. 33. Shaya took advantage of the chance to mock her younger brother's colleague.

"Zero points, Ev?" she wondered. "You've got to be kidding me."

"Shaya," Monsky introduced himself. "They don't keep the assists there."

The jab stung Monsky's pride despite his deadpan answer. Prior to him, Kobe was named captain. Shaya was now breaking his stones? How many times did Monsky need to be informed that he wasn't on the same level as Kobe? However, the sting didn't last long. As the teams' captains met with the referees at half-court before another game later that month, Kobe ducked out, ran back to the huddle, and grabbed Monsky and Stewart. "Come on," he said to them. "We're going to the circle." Monsky and Stewart joined him there before every game from then until the end of the season. "That's always stuck with me," Monsky subsequently remarked. "Who cares if you're the captain of a high school team? You exchange handshakes with the other captains. It's insignificant. But that counts to a seventeen-year-old kid, and him going out of his way to bring us in was truly something I appreciated. I never got to tell him about it."

A rip-roaring start—victories in their first five games—hinted that the La Salle Explorers might be regaining relevance in Philadelphia basketball and, in a sense, in the country. Instead, the club stumbled to a .500 record, 13-13, before the Midwestern Collegiate Conference tournament in 1995. The mediocre season was a microcosm of the program's circumstances and poor decision making, with students and alumni apathetic about seeing the team face opponents from Illinois and Wisconsin, opponents with no rivalries or emotional ties to La Salle and East Coast basketball fans. The Civic Center could hold ten thousand spectators; the Explorers were lucky to draw two thousand for a game. One night, from the press box, a Philadelphia reporter remarked, "You know, if you put everybody in this place on the court, no one would get called for three seconds."

Speedy Morris' decision to hire Joe Bryant as an assistant coach was also not paying off financially. The players liked him—who didn't like Joe on a superficial, human level?—but his coaching duties and commitment to his job frequently seemed to him to be less essential than Kobe's upcoming game. During one practice, when the Explorers were working on an offensive set play, Joe moved into the centre of the drill and executed a hard pick on senior Paul Burke, the team's leading point guard, sending Burke to the floor.

"What the hell are you doing, Joe?" Morris asked.

With each triumph, every magnificent Kobe moment, the notion that basketball was only of passing interest to Lower Merion's school body or surrounding community faded. The school's tone and culture were changing, removing the arrogance and intimidation associated with athletics, and he was at the epicentre of the transformation. Dan Gross, a member of Kobe's class who went on to become a gossip columnist for the Philadelphia Daily News, was a punk-music fan who had not followed any of the school's sports teams, preferring instead to join his friends for concerts at fire halls, church basements, or the Trocadero, a historic theatre in Philadelphia's Chinatown. "But there was something about this," he said. "It was contagious knowing there was someone so talented at your school." Watching Kobe play at that level, crushing everyone in high school, was what got us to pay attention for the first time." One of Maher's first orders as principal was to abolish Freshman Day and its attendant hazing, and it helped that in the boys' basketball program, which was quickly becoming the most popular sport on campus, the head coach had never allowed hazing in the first place, and the best player, universally regarded as respectful of teachers and students, had never participated in it. "Sports had gotten run down some at Lower Merion, for whatever reason," Maher explained, "and I think that made it OK again." It was acceptable to try out for sports. You were not required to attend a private school and participate in sports. You could stay and play at Lower Merion." With the annual three-on-three Hoop It Up competition coming, and Kobe's teams having won it three years in a row, Maher approached him outside the principal's office one morning and inquired whether he'd be competing. "I don't know," Kobe admitted. Instead of dominating the event again and leaving the other students dissatisfied by the predictable outcome, Maher recommended that Kobe referee instead. He concurred. "He understood who he was," Maher explained.

There was little doubt about it when it came to basketball. Sterling Carroll, the track team captain, sought to recruit Kobe to run track after he had pondered pranking him on Freshman Day but decided against it. "At the very least, you could do the high jump," Carroll said. But Kobe was uninterested. "He was one of the most focused people I've ever seen," Carroll said, "but he was strictly focused on basketball." Jimmy Black, an assistant coach at Notre Dame, came to a practice one afternoon to scout Kobe. He then introduced himself to Kobe, who was polite but unenthusiastic. Egan asked Kobe if he knew who Black was when he offered him a lift home that night. "Yeah, assistant at Notre Dame," Kobe answered, slumping in the front seat. Egan pointed out that there's more to him than that. Black had started at point guard for North Carolina's 1982 national championship team... with Michael Jordan. Kobe sat up abruptly, a rush of adrenaline coursing through him. "He played with Mike?" he inquired. "Oh my goodness! What happened to him? "Can we go speak with him?" He had no interest in playing basketball for and earning a degree from the nation's most prestigious Catholic university. Kobe valued Black's experience with and proximity to Jordan. "He wasn't really interested in Notre Dame," Egan remarked, "or Jimmy Black, for that matter."

Kobe was still learning and investigating everything else in his life— his identity, intelligence, and social life. Only in specific conditions and scenarios, with specific people, would he let down his guard and open up, a posture that his friends and family believed arose from his awareness of difference from other teenagers, from his recognition that he needed time to transition into American culture. "When he came from Italy," remarked his student and friend Susan Freeland, "we could be rude, talk fast, and talk over each other." We're from Philadelphia, after all. That is not typical in Italy. He was still learning the language. He became quieter. He came across as thoughtful to us." It would be easy to believe that his basketball future was the only thing on his mind, that his fixation with the sport consumed every area of his life. It is more realistic to view greatness in the sport as a goal toward which he kept himself oriented, and to realise that he would marshal whatever resources and abilities were available to him to assist him on the journey. Getting after-school tutoring for a geometry subject was a challenge rather than a nuisance. Egan inquired as to how things were going. "Good, really good," Kobe exclaimed. "This shit is a lot of fun." His SAT score of

1080, when combined with his athletic prowess, did not qualify him for admission to Duke, Notre Dame, or any Ivy League university. Instead, it was a reflection of who he was and what he might do in the future. He could attend whatever college he wanted and succeed there. "It's like the saying, too much of one thing can be bad, right?" his cousin John Cox added. "Not for him, because you already knew it was his passion." He discovered his love early on, but he was still well-rounded. He was reading. He was a voracious reader. Everything should be read. It was more focused on masters of their profession, to examine what they accomplished and how they got ahead by picking up minor things. He was still doing it for basketball, but it wasn't the only reason. He was reading to improve his ability to communicate and educate himself. He would still relax and spend time with his family because he wasn't compromising by going out and attending parties. That kept him grounded enough that we didn't think he was OD'ing on the ball. It didn't appear to be an overdose. He worked hard, but he maintained a sense of balance."

He would attend Student Voice meetings when he could, going by the library to ask Katrina Christmas, the organisation's moderator, what issues were on the agenda for the next meeting. When he did show up, it wasn't as if he was taking over and running the meeting, but he would sit at a desk and stretch his long legs into the aisle, raise his hand to contribute to the discussion and make suggestions, joke and laugh, and Christmas appreciated that, despite his devotion to basketball, he would make the effort to be there. Deirdre Bobb, a student voice member a year younger than Kobe, noticed that Kobe usually seemed to have at least one lady following him into meetings or from class to class. He enjoyed the attention, but he was modest about it, which Bobb appreciated. Christmas also noticed the following: Several Black male pupils, some from West Philly and some from Ardmore, disliked Kobe. They questioned and doubted his racial credibility. He couldn't get away from it on the basketball court or in the corridors of his high school.

"Jealousy—they were jealous," said Christmas. "They were saying, 'He don't know how to play no ball because he'd never played ball in the streets.'" He was playing ball, and they were playing street ball. 'When you play street ball, you're a different animal. You are shoved. You are knocked out. You become bloodthirsty.' He was described as an adorable person. I could understand what they were saying, but they didn't understand his heart.

"It comes with being Black and having to enter a different type of circle." You always feel the need to prove yourself. I'm sure it made him sad on occasion. After a while, that stuff gets to you. It truly does. It really hits home that others will judge you based on what they see on the outside rather than what they see on the inside. Now you must do anything you can to demonstrate to them, 'Hey, dude, I'm human just like you.'"

He was the type of child who resisted categorization, who thrived in being different, who was content to connect with anyone through whatever passion or trait they shared, as long as he could channel it back to his compulsion, to the thing he loved most. Student Voice's choir celebrate Black History Month in February 1995 by performing a concert containing the music of Aretha Franklin, Lena Horne, and Cab Calloway. After hearing Bobb sing, Kobe approached her and asked if she would sing the national anthem before a basketball game. Bobb was initially apprehensive, but after the first performance, Kobe insisted that she sing the anthem before every Lower Merion game, and that he would not step onto the field unless he first heard her voice. "It became so passionate," Bobb said, "that I made it a point to attend every game, even away games." 'Listen, I have a female in that crowd with a fantastic voice,' he would tell the officials. I'd like her to sing and start the game before the rest of the team comes.' "I just felt incredibly honoured." Bobb would close her eyes until the final sections of the anthem, when she would open them. She'd always find the basketball team and catch a glimpse of Kobe, his head bowed and his eyes closed. "He would open his eyes and give me the biggest smile and two thumbs up," she said after she finished. You're all set, Deirdre. I'm all set to go.

The Aces' victory at Colesville was their twelfth in a row, and the streak would last another nine games, reaching twenty-one, lifting the program to a level unimaginable to its coaches, players, and supporters. Chester hovered over the entire neighbourhood; the Clippers had lost five games, but they had played such a strong schedule that no one, least of all Kobe and Downer, had any doubts about how good they truly were. Nonetheless, the team's confidence was boosted by the variety and causes of their victories. Griffin scored twenty-five and twenty-four points in back-to-back games, the first an eleven-point victory over Glen Mills, the second a twelve-point victory over Haverford in which Kobe spent much of the game spitting clumps of phlegm into a paper bag and shivering so much as he sat on the bench that Pam draped her red shawl over him. Despite this, he managed to score 36 points. Pangrazio upset Marple Newtown in the fourth quarter by sinking eight consecutive free throws. Lower Merion defeated Ridley 76-70, and Kobe scored 42 points to lead the squad to its first league championship in more than a decade. "We felt like this was going to be our year," he continued. Dave Rosenberg, whose parents were not originally from the area, was unfamiliar with high school basketball in the Philadelphia area and its rivalries. He was perplexed to see Downer, Egan, and the other Aces coaches reacting to Ridley's victory as if it were the Super Bowl, and he wasn't alone.

"Ridley was in the league," Rosenberg added, "and Kobe said,'Ridley's not the one you want to beat.'"

Lower Merion's final regular-season game, versus St. Anthony in Jersey City, was everything but conventional. The Friars were 19-2 and consistently ranked among the top ten high school teams in the country, and while Downer expected that facing them on their turf, on their terms, would be a good test of his team's talent and toughness, the game tested the Aces' resolve more than he could have imagined. Stewart was out due to illness, and in the second quarter, Monsky raced in on a partial breakaway and collided with a St. Anthony player as he jumped for a basket. He fell and chipped a bone in his left wrist while bracing himself as he descended, forcing him to miss the rest of the game.

Hurley had never seen Kobe play in person; despite having a slew of pals, tipsters, and hangers-on throughout his basketball career, he only had one scouting report on him. "We didn't have much information," Hurley admitted, "other than he was a great individual player." Hurley's teams exclusively played man-to-man defence, and in order to excite them and make the challenge of containing Kobe appear more manageable, he exhorted them in the huddle, We've had a lot of guys better than that man walk through our doors throughout the years. Hurley's remark was misinterpreted by Egan as an insult to Kobe, but the Friars set out to prove their coach accurate. They restricted Kobe to 22 points and never trailed in their 83-67 victory, and the cost for Lower Merion went beyond the final score. Monsky would have to play with his left arm in a cast that he kept wrapped in Styrofoam to protect his wounded wrist, and the district playoffs began just two nights later. The Aces finished 21-3 and were the No. 2 seed in the 32-team tournament, trailing only Chester. But they wouldn't be at full strength, and Kobe would be under greater pressure than ever before against the opponents they wanted to beat.

I decided to spend most of my free time—nights, weekends—going to gyms and playing basketball. By myself.

—KOBE BRYANT

CHAPTER 2

THE PIT

There was no such thing as a short road trip for the Philadelphia 76ers in 1994-95, and when John Lucas, their coach and general manager, returned from one in late February—three games in five days, all on the West Coast—he was exhausted and bemused by a surprising assertion from his wife, Debbie. Those Sixers were dreadful, the kind of terrible that is only funny in retrospect. They'd go 24-58 and finish sixth out of the seven teams in the NBA's Atlantic Division; in many ways, their philosophy and culture were shamefully backward. They would field nineteen players in at least one game. Shawn Bradley, the No. 2 overall choice in the 1993 draft, struggled so hard to gain upper-body strength and weight that the training staff would bring cheesecakes to shootarounds and practices for him. He'd stuff his face, then puke.

Lucas might have been the ideal coach for such a team based on temperament, philosophy, and personal background. He was optimistic to the point of Pollyanna, believing genuinely that every human being was capable of redemption, no matter how terrible or detrimental his or her misdeeds were. He was a recovering drug and alcohol user whose troubles dogged and nearly wrecked his fourteen-year NBA playing career. When you're passed out on the bathroom floor and your children have to step over you in the morning, you learn humility, he used to say. He was open to seeing things in people and basketball players that others might not—all desirable characteristics, even if they didn't make him a particularly successful coach. The Sixers had lost all three games on the trip, the most recent by thirty points against the Nuggets in Denver. The defeats were wearing on Lucas, but there were some bright spots in the scenario. Moving to Philadelphia allowed him to strengthen his bond with his University of Maryland backcourt mate, Mo Howard, and he and his family had settled in a pleasant neighbourhood with an excellent school district just west of the city. He and Debbie had known each other since they were adolescent lovebirds in Durham, North Carolina, and she had always told him he was the best high school basketball player she'd ever seen. However, as Lucas went through his front door, he saw that he had been pushed down a rung on his wife's hoops hierarchy.

"I've finally seen a high school basketball player who is better than you," she remarked.

Despite a small, unstated hint, he had no idea who Debbie was talking about: Tarvia, their daughter, was a junior at Lower Merion. Despite their lack of postseason experience and Monsky's broken wrist, the Aces breezed through the first two rounds of the district tournament, then relied on Kobe for 35 points—one in the first quarter, six in the second, eleven in the third, and eighteen in the fourth—to defeat Norristown, 75-70, in the quarterfinals. (In addition, Kobe had twelve rebounds and eight blocked shots.) The win guaranteed them a spot in the state playoffs... and a date with a familiar rival five days later: Coatesville. Despite Downer's goal-setting and lectures to the squad about aiming to play in the semifinals at the Palestra, most of the players had no idea what the district tournament was. This is what they knew: We have practice tomorrow if we win. Someone please bring doughnuts.... Oh, this game has standing room only? Cool. What about the next one? What is the Palestra? Awesome. Everything was new and exciting. The Kobe experience broadened everyone's understanding of what Lower Merion basketball was, how the team could and should play, and what it could achieve. Downer could feel it in the plays he called in the huddle.

Attempt an alley-oop. Downer had previously hesitated to design one because he wasn't sure he had a player capable of catching a pass near the rim and dunking the ball while still hanging in the air; and two, because the alley-oop requires such high levels of timing and precision, especially between two high school players. "A bad alley-oop pass will devastate a play," he explained. "That's the crucial link." But with Kobe, all it needed was a good back pick on his man and a pass that drifted within two feet of the hoop for an alley-oop to work. Kobe would be released. He could catch it with just one hand. He'd hammer it home. "I remember driving in my car one day and thinking, 'There's no such thing as a bad alley-oop pass for this kid,'" Downer explained. "He caught one behind his head and threw it down once." 'There's no way this can be different from Grant Hill or Penny Hardaway,' I realised. 'How can it be any other way?'" And what is impossible when you have Grant Hill or Penny Hardaway on your team... when you have Michael Jordan in your gym?

The inverse of that question, of course, terrified Downer: What would happen if Kobe wasn't there? He got his answer from Coatesville. A Philadelphia Inquirer writer called William Duffy, the associate administrator for academic affairs at Roman Catholic High School, the night before the game. Yes, Duffy had heard the rumours that Kobe Bryant would move to Roman for his senior year. However, any pupil transferring would have to go through his office, and the Bryants had not contacted him. "My understanding of the situation," Duffy explained to the reporter, "is that it's not true." Downer was a little concerned by the Roman discourse. The fact that Donnie Carr, Kobe's friend and rival from the Sonny Hill League, joined Roman added credence to the reports, and Downer had been on the lookout for Kobe-is-transferring rumours since Kobe was in eighth grade.

A high school basketball game lasts 32 minutes. Lucas saw Kobe for exactly 27 minutes and 22 seconds against Coatesville. During that time, he witnessed Kobe score 26 points. He saw him score ten points in the third quarter to cut the Red Raiders' lead to ten. He saw Monsky make a couple of nice passes that Kobe turned into thunderous dunks. And, with 4:38 seconds left in regulation and the Aces behind by one, he witnessed Kobe foul out. Downer no longer had the option of alley-oops. "We have to play defence," a helpless Kobe shouted in the huddle as the two senior captains, Stewart and Monsky, pushed their colleagues to seize the moment. Every morning, they read Kobe's name in the box score, Kobe's name throughout the game, quotes from Kobe, and quotes about Kobe. So … Was it a one-man show or not? "We're going to have to win without him," Stewart remarked. "This is our chance to prove we're better than him."

They held Coatesville scoreless for the next two and a half minutes, building a five-point lead and never letting the Red Raiders get any closer, Kobe raising his arms in a V after the 72-65 victory and Griffin rushing to wrap his arms around him, despite Griffin's tender left ankle, which he sprained during the game. Rip Hamilton, who had fifteen points at halftime, had only seven in the second half; Egan's pressure defence was effective even without Kobe in the post. Downer later commended the Aces' tenacity—"A lot of teams would have been devastated if a player of that calibre fouled out," he remarked, putting an end to the Kobe-transfer rumours. "It isn't true," he explained. "He has a lot left to do at Lower Merion," probably beginning with capturing a district championship in 48 hours. On a Friday night at the DuPont Pavilion at Villanova. In opposition to Chester.

Meanwhile, John Lucas was on his way home from the Palestra. He knew he wouldn't be able to attend the district championship game. The Sixers were slated to play the New Jersey Nets in East Rutherford that night. Besides, he'd had enough of it. A basketball court was at the heart of the William Penn projects in Chester. The court, made of concrete and asphalt, fell into the ground like a pit. Boys, male teenagers, and men began playing there early in the morning and continued until the thick veil of night fell over them. They selected sides and picked each other up full-court, as the oldest among them offered memories steeped in their city's history and legacy. The youngest among them were chastised for settling for a jump shot, that nobody deserved to wear the orange-and-black uniform of the Chester Clippers and represent that high school and this community by playing weak-ass basketball. Those kids learnt in the pit that the sport may be as important to their survival and flourishing as their pounding hearts. The frightening pops of gunfire and foreboding blares of police sirens, the dreadful sounds inherent in their lives, would become mute to their ears for a moment in the pit. There was nothing to fear in the pit. In Chester, you went to the pit to climb out.

Chester had degenerated into an exemplar of post industrial decline from a booming city hard on the Delaware River in the mid-1950s, with a diversified population of about seventy thousand citizens and a vibrant main street and an economy fuelled by companies that constructed ships, trains, and machinery. The town had become an urban cautionary tale as a result of local political corruption, suburbanization of the region and the subsequent white flight, redlining, race riots, and blockbusting. Chester's population shrank to less than 40,000 persons, 80 percent of whom were Black. It was the poorest city in Pennsylvania and America's second-most deadly city. Its housing projects were "open-air drug markets," according to author Christopher Mele, and in the 1980s, the William Penn residences ``became [a] one-stop hub for cocaine and heroin distribution, sales, and open consumption." Simply put, Chester was the inverse of Lower Merion. That they did. Throughout the first half, the teams traded baskets, with Kobe scoring fourteen points and the Aces struggling to keep up with the Clippers' rapid, full-ninety-four-foot pace. Ray Carroll, a Fordham forward on a full basketball scholarship, drove toward the hoop in the first quarter, and Monsky stayed strong in front of him in an attempt to take charge and draw an offensive foul. Carroll took off to shoot and collided with Monsky, knocking him over, and landing with all of his weight on Monkey's face. Monsky stayed in the game until the third quarter, when he and Stewart fouled out, his arm in a cast and one of his eyes a swirl of black and purple. Downer stood up, ripped off his sport coat, and threw it into the bleachers after a 12-2 Chester run. It landed in the lap of his best friend. The game was becoming out of control. When the Chester lead reached eighteen points in the fourth quarter, Downer removed Kobe and the rest of his starters and sent out an all-sub lineup, kids who only played when the game's fate was certain. He then turned to face Egan on the bench.

"What should we do?" he inquired.

"I don't know," Egan responded. The ultimate score, 77-50, was unsurprising given the disparity between the two programs. Lower Merion had a total of twenty-nine turnovers. Linehan had six steals himself. "We were injured, and we weren't ready," stated Monsky. "It was an environment we'd never played in before, and Chester had probably played there a million times." Even Kobe could only tip the scales so far. He trudged out of the Pavilion weary, having scored twenty-three points and gained a better grasp of what he and the Aces were up against the next year if they were to win a district championship. "They just wore us down," he said, adding that the only consolation for him and his teammates, particularly Monsky, Stewart, and the other seniors, was that the state finals started in less than a week. The La Salle University men's basketball season, as well as the team's tenure in the Midwestern Collegiate Conference, came to an end 550 miles to the west, in Dayton, Ohio, with a 54-46 loss to Wisconsin-Green Bay. With a record of 13-14. Another season in which the Explorers were not one of the sixty-four teams who qualified for the NCAA tournament. If there was to be a comeback, the following season promised to be the tipping point. La Salle was leaving the MCC to compete in a more geographically suited conference, the Atlantic 10, alongside Temple, St. Joseph's, and other institutions. With that move, the program's issues appeared to be nothing that Kobe's presence couldn't remedy... if he chose to go there... and there were already forces at work, working independently to make that happen.

Where would they rather be? Basketball was in the hands of Kobe Bryant, which all the Aces, from Downer to Egan to every player on the roster to every player's father, considered to be the safest spot on the planet. The score was 49-49 in the second round of the Pennsylvania Class AAAA tournament at Liberty High School in Bethlehem. The rival team—Hazleton, from the state's northeast— and its fans had taken over the majority of the gym, comparable in size and excitement to Chester's, as disparate as they could be in other ways. "The crowd," Stewart observed, "was not pro-minority." The atmosphere was heated, and the Aces' performance in the final minutes of the fourth quarter was sloppy. With a one-point lead, they fanned out and tried to bleed the clock, and one of their players,

Tariq Wilson, was holding the ball in one arm against his hip when he just... dropped it, and it slid out of bounds. But Kobe had the ball in a tie game, and he had thirty-three points, despite the fact that Hazleton had been double-teaming and trapping him the entire night, just as the Cougars were now with the clock ticking down from:10 to:09 to:08, two players right up on him, waving their hands and arms to distract him, obstruct his view, or maybe bat the ball out of his hands for a steal on the off chance that Kobe, in But such folly was unthinkable now, for the ball was at the safest spot on the planet ... until it didn't. Until one of those Hazleton players snatched the ball from Kobe's grasp. Until there was a rush for it, and Hazleton guard Ryan Leib grabbed it and dribbled frantically to the basket, desperate to beat the buzzer with a game-winning layup... and getting there... and flipping the ball up toward the rim... and missing. Overtime. Lower Merion's bench should have let out a huge sigh of relief that the season had not ended, a calm team taking charge of the game. That was not the case. Perhaps the sight of Kobe's error, his frailty in such a crucial moment, was too unsettling and disorienting. Hazleton kept double-teaming him. He couldn't see the basket clearly. There was no one else to pick up the slack. The Aces failed to score in the five-minute overtime round; on their penultimate possession, Kobe grabbed a rebound and dribbled the length of the floor... into three Hazleton players. Lower Merion lost the game, 64-59, when he dropped the ball. Downer then looked around the changing room. Only sneezes could be heard. "Does anyone have anything to say?" he inquired. Evan Monsky and Guy Stewart did. Neither spoke for more than a minute. We'd all been playing together since we were kids, and it seemed surreal to think about how bad our team had been and how we were now playing in the state playoffs in a packed arena. I'll miss basketball, but you guys will be missed even more.

Kobe couldn't speak at first. Finally, he began repeating the same two words: "I'm sorry."

The rest of those minutes in the locker room at Liberty High School are a haze in the minds of those who were there. Gregg Downer recalls wondering what Kobe would say next, if he would keep the

28

romantic tone of the event, and witnessing Kobe deliver a sermon devoid of sympathy. Those are fantastic stories, and we'll miss the seniors, for which I apologise. But let me make one thing clear to everyone in this room: This will never happen again on my watch. Stewart recalls Kobe's apologies to the squad and his pledge to his older teammates, who were graduating, that he would pay them back. Brendan Pettit recalls his astonishment at the loss, as well as his realisation of the expectation that would be placed on the squad the following year, when he realised he could be a part of something extraordinary. Egan remembers only Kobe crying. There was no determined, meaningful discourse. There will be no defiance. Just those two words, again and over. I apologise. Perhaps that is the reaction that everyone should have expected from Kobe Bryant at that moment in his life: he was still five months away from his seventeenth birthday, and nothing else mattered as much to him as his own image of himself. During his outstanding junior season, he averaged 31.1 points and 10.4 rebounds per game. He had brought his team to a level it hadn't reached in years. But if he wasn't a district champion, a state champion, or the best, who was he, and who did people think he was? I'm sorry. I'm sorry. I'm sorry

People made a point to tell me how shocked they were that I was this seventeen-year-old kid who was so sure of himself and confident in his abilities that I put myself in this unique position, to choose among the top colleges in the country or the NBA.

—KOBE BRYANT

CHAPTER 3

MYTH AND REALITY

Joe Bryant was an "awesome guy" to John Kunzier, La Salle University's women's volleyball coach, during their time on campus together, friendly anytime they chatted in the athletic offices, hallways, and the third-floor gymnasium of Hayman Hall. At La Salle, volleyball was not a top-tier sport. Kunzier's teams had stumbled to a 17-78 record in his first three years as coach, and despite the anticipated shift to the Atlantic 10, he did not expect the institution to start lavishing money on his club. The NCAA allowed its member institutions to have up to twelve volleyball players on scholarship. La Salle's sports budget allowed Kunzier to have four. It had given him four, at least until the late spring of 1994, when athletic director Bob Mullen and senior women's administrator Kathy McNally gave him what had to have been wonderful news.

McNally informed Kunzier, "You got another scholarship player." Shaya, a six-foot-two middle blocker, is her name. Kunzier had never solicited Shaya Bryant to play volleyball at La Salle, nor had anyone ever addressed the notion of her doing so with him. He stated that "there was no money" in the budget. "There was nothing there. But, out of nowhere, I got an extra player who wasn't in any of my plans. I had no idea who she was." She only played one season, in the fall of 1995, and she led the club in blocks. But the Explorers' record didn't improve much (to 4-27, up from 3-30 the previous season), and Shaya only stayed at La Salle for one year. "Shaya was a lovely young lady," said Kunzier, who retired after that season, "not the toughest player I ever had, but athletic and gifted and really, really sweet and nice." Don't get him wrong: He was delighted to have her and to coach her. Given the team's troubles, he would have welcomed anyone who possessed Shaya's qualities. It was the situation's obvious opportunism that worried him.

"I believe La Salle was willing to do whatever it took to get Kobe at the time," Kunzier said. "They paid Joe's salary." They were willing to give Kobe a full ride, just as they did Shaya. It was a move by Bob Mullen. When I arrived, the place was a shambles. It was a complete disaster. I believe Bob saw Kobe as his saviour, and this was going to be his great comeback."

The worth of Shaya Bryant's sports scholarship—tuition, lodging and board, a meal plan, and a twelve-credit course load—would have been around $20,000 for the one year she spent at La Salle. But it wasn't the only price Mullen was willing to pay to bring Kobe back to school. Morris's two key assistant coaches, Joe Mihalich and Joe Bryant, were paid $34,000 and $32,000, respectively, entering the summer of 1995. Mullen informed Morris one day that he had negotiated a $50,000 raise for Joe Bryant. That's fantastic, Morris said to Mullen. But if Jellybean gets $50,000, Mihalich must get $52,000. Mullen erupted in rage and bewilderment. Are you insane? Do you realise you're putting your neck on the line if you don't get Kobe? Morris was unconcerned. Mihalich had three children and had worked for Morris since 1986. Morris mentioned a loyalty issue to Mullen. Joe Mihalich is my man. Joe Bryant will not get a boost unless you give him one. Mullen stormed out of Morris' office, furious. He informed Morris the following day that Joe Mihalich's new salary was $52,000.

Mullen had reason to assume those bread crumbs would lure Kobe, because Kobe was considering La Salle... under certain situations and scenarios. The fact that the university was joining the Atlantic 10 piqued his interest—the conference already had natural rivalries with Temple and St. Joseph's for the Explorers—as did the chance of playing with Lari Ketner, a six-foot-ten centre from Roman Catholic High School. Ketner, a grade ahead of Kobe, had verbally committed to La Salle in the spring, but he had signed no papers and made no official commitments. Part of him still wanted to leave his choices open, and one of the reasons he was waiting to commit totally to Morris and La Salle was to have a clearer feel of what Kobe's college decision would be. When Kobe and Ketner teamed up for pickup games at Hayman, they dominated the players who were already on La Salle's roster—Kobe knifing into the lane at will, throwing alley-oop passes to Ketner for dunks, looking at the college kids' faces and recognizing that they were agog with the possibility of what the Explorers could be with him and Ketner. If you tell me you're going to La Salle, Ketner said, I'll sign tomorrow. Consider working together to turn the program around.

Kobe, on the other hand, couldn't and wouldn't give Ketner any assurances, not just because he didn't want to make a promise he couldn't keep, but because Joe had a pipe-dream plan that, if the circumstances were right and he could pull it off, would ensure that Kobe ended up at La Salle. Neither Joe nor Kobe were positive it would happen, but the plan was predicated on a series of occurrences that, to Joe, seemed to be becoming more likely by the day. For the first time in program history, the Explorers suffered two consecutive losing seasons, and their record had deteriorated in each of the previous three years. Alumni and administrators were growing restless and impatient with Morris, as Mullen had made abundantly plain. Another bad season, Joe reasoned, and Morris's dismissal would be a certain conclusion, and the institution would be forced to hire... Joe. There were already rumours on the breeze, an open secret in some circles, a complete secret to Morris. "They really talked about Joe getting the job at La Salle," stated Sam Rines Jr. "And, obviously, if Joe had gotten the job, Kobe would have gone to La Salle."

It's not just Kobe Joe had put together his own version of the "Fab Five," the renowned 1991 Michigan recruiting class that led the Wolverines to national titles in 1992 and 1993, based on his contacts and Kobe's travels and friendships on the AAU circuit: Kobe; Rip Hamilton, who had become friends with Kobe and had joined the Sam Rines All-Stars; Shaheen Holloway; Lester Earl; and Jermaine O'Neal, who was born in Eau Claire, South Carolina. Joe was confident that he could persuade the majority of them, if not all four, to join Kobe at La Salle. He was already recruiting them, talking them up to Morris and Mihalich. He had no doubt that if he could tell them, "I'll be your head coach," they'd commit right away. Neither did Kobe. He played with them, against them, and discussed this same subject with them over the phone. Who wouldn't want to play for his father? Ketner finally backed out of his oral pledge to La Salle and transferred to the University of Massachusetts in Boston. But those four people would have loved to play for Joe—Donnie Carr would have loved to, too, and what if they could bring him along?—It wouldn't have mattered if they were at La Salle, with its dingy practice gym and a string of losses in recent years. They couldn't compete with the Fab Five. They'd be better, and they'd just have to remain for a year before leaving for the NBA, and Kobe wouldn't have to look for a college coach who would look after him, a college coach who would nurture him. He was going to get one. He'd have his father. Morris, Morris, Morris... Was Speedy Morris going to be that kind of Kobe coach?... When Joe suggested that La Salle recruit Sharif Butler out of junior college, Speedy Morris said, "No, we don't think he's good enough." "It really hurt the family deep down inside," Joe admitted. "That means he didn't really understand the Bryant family at the time." ... Speedy Morris, who thought Kobe wasn't good enough to play in the NBA—not that he shouldn't, but that he couldn't. "How am I going to trust this guy to raise my son if he doesn't think he's good enough?" Joe wondered. ... Speedy Morris, his rage on a hair trigger, so enraged by a bad play or a bad call that he couldn't help but stomp his feet like a toddler demanding a toy his parents refused to buy, his pants sometimes splitting, his voice reaching a higher pitch and ringing throughout the Civic Center... Kobe had witnessed a handful of those mushroom clouds. There was a period in Joe's coaching career at La Salle when he would have been overjoyed if Kobe chose to play there. But that was it: the decision was always Kobe's, and he thought Speedy yelled too much at his guys. He told Joe and Pam the truth, and they didn't mind.

The blueprints and promises that Kobe Bryant and others close to him had been following and chasing since he was a newborn came to fruition in the spring and summer of 1995. As dynamic and dominant as he was for Lower Merion, and as much as winning a state title propelled him, his junior season had become the Remington Park pickup games with his middle and high school teammates. Pitting himself simply against youngsters who weren't at his level as ballplayers would provide no creative friction or challenge for him. "He was never in the moment," claimed Sonny Vaccaro. "He was always thinking about the next moment." It's also worth noting that Kobe's heightened urgency and success in refining his game coincided with a seismic event in professional sports. After a seventeen-month retirement/hiatus from basketball, Michael Jordan scored nineteen points for the Chicago Bulls in a loss to the Indiana Pacers on March 19, 1995, just four days after the Aces' season-ending loss to Hazleton in the state finals. MJ was back, and his presence gave Kobe another goal to go for, another marathon finish-line tape to break. Only a few outsiders could see what his endgame was.

For example, Villanova assistant coach Paul Hewitt decided to drive to Lower Merion to see him practise one day that spring. He was accompanied by Jonathan Haynes, the Wildcats' starting point guard, who knew very little about Kobe and had never met him. Hewitt had been courting Kobe in the hopes of adding him to a stellar freshmen class that included Tim Thomas. Kobe was intrigued by the prospect of teaming up with Thomas and tearing the Big East apart. In theory, two of the Wildcats' top scorers—guards Kerry Kittles, a projected NBA lottery pick, and Eric Eberz—would graduate before Kobe came, opening up positions in the starting lineup for him and Thomas straight away. College basketball wouldn't be ready for two guys like me and Timmy on the same team, Kobe reasoned, and because his uncle Chubby Cox had played for the Wildcats, he saw Villanova as a possible destination. Hewitt left with his chest puffed after Kobe had what he subsequently described as "an unbelievable practice" and chatted with him and Haynes. Hewitt was certain that Kobe would stay on the Main Line for college. That's one hell of a recruiting class. Nobody is beyond our reach.

Except Haynes was mocking him.

"What's so funny?" Hewitt inquired.

"Coach," Haynes remarked, "you have no shot at getting this guy."

"What exactly do you mean?"

"Coach, he's not going to college." He's on his way to the NBA."

Haynes' insight into Kobe's thoughts struck Hewitt like lightning. "For a college kid to say that about a high school kid, that's when I started to realise this dude must be something different," Hewitt recounted. "Kobe and I had a lot of chats. I didn't realise it at the time, but he was always asking about the game. He was always curious about the game and loved talking about basketball; he was always looking for facts and knowledge. At the moment, you believe he's a seventeen-year-old kid, and it's great that he's participating in the conversation. You learn later in life that this kid was on a journey to be exceptional."

To grasp Kobe's mindset and trajectory, one did not have to be of Kobe's generation. From that night at the Palestra, that playoff game against Coatesville, John Lucas saw Kobe in the same way that Kobe saw himself: not at sixteen, but at twenty-one, twenty-two, and beyond. To guarantee his Sixers players stayed in shape and maintained an NBA-quality competitive environment during the league's offseason, Lucas urged them to participate in regular, informal pickup games between pros and college players in all of Philadelphia's recognizable locations. The Sixers' official practice facility was St. Joseph's University's Fieldhouse, and Lucas entrusted his old friend Mo Howard to oversee the two practices per day, from 9 a.m. until 7 p.m. Lucas called the Bryants and invited Kobe to the exercises, and he gave Howard a directive: I don't care how you put the teams together, but Kobe has to participate. If Kobe can and wants to play, he will. That's the end of the narrative.

Even before his high school season concluded, Kobe phoned Phil Martelli, the St. Joseph's men's basketball coach in his first year, and asked if he could work out at the Fieldhouse. Martelli added Kobe's name on the guest list, where it remained until the following school year began in September. "If he played for Lower Merion on Tuesdays and Fridays," Martelli explained, "he would come into our gym on Mondays, Wednesdays, and Thursdays." So accepting Lucas' invitation didn't require Kobe to disrupt his meticulous, jam-packed schedule—pickup and practice, workouts and weight-training during the week; AAU tournaments and all-star camps on weekends—and it gave him a chance to bond with his carpool mate, Emory Dabney, during the five-to-ten-minute drive to St. Joe's. Dabney, two years younger than Kobe and sensitive and high-strung, had spent his freshman year at the Woodlynde School in Strafford, PA, a day school for adolescents with learning difficulties and challenges. He had been the point player on Woodlynde's basketball team and had played summer league ball with Kobe and the Aces, when he met Gregg Downer, and had turned down many scholarship offers from private high schools in order to move to Lower Merion. During those summer games, he had also captured Lucas' attention, and Lucas was so taken with Dabney that he offered him the opportunity to be the youngest player in a gym full of guys. If it was unusual for Kobe, who was entering his senior year, to work out with pros and experienced college athletes, having a child who was only a few weeks shy of his fifteenth birthday do the same may sound absurd. But, before meeting Lucas and Kobe, Dabney had discovered a basketball mentor who eclipsed them both in terms of stature: Cory Erving, Julius's son, had been Dabney's greatest buddy at Woodlynde. Julius would volunteer to play one-on-one against Dabney whenever he visited the Ervings' home in Villanova. "We'd mess around," Dabney explained. "'OK, you want to see what defence is like in the NBA Finals?'" I replied, 'Yeah.' I couldn't even function. For years and years, I would become better, and he'd say, 'You're going to start playing in front of bigger crowds. This is what it will be like.' And I never hesitated to perform in front of a large crowd."

Cory Erving died in a vehicle accident in 2000, when he was nineteen, and Dabney is still dealing with the loss of two of his closest friends at such a young age. Kobe would pick up Dabney in the Bryants' old white BMW and, later, in a new light green Toyota Land Cruiser for their first workouts together; at St. Joe's, they would focus on aerobic training, mostly running on a track inside the Fieldhouse. "Kobe was always like a big brother," said Dabney. "He'd offer me advice." Off the court, I spent a lot of time with him. He spent a lot of time at my house. I was at his place. He simply wanted to see you improve and succeed, even with your homework and grades. He was all over you about it. He was simply a wonderful person to be around at that age. I get emotional just thinking about it. Even though he was only seventeen or eighteen at the time, he laid the groundwork for you to be successful in life. You got that vibe just by being around him." However, after the 1995 NBA draft came place in late June, the tone of those workouts shifted from the monotony of everyday sprints and exercises to a type of basketball mythology that is still alive and well today.

The expectation was that Jerry Stackhouse would be The Next Big Thing, either during his undergraduate career at North Carolina or after the Sixers selected him with the No. 3 pick in the 1995 draft. Michael Jordan was both gratifying and absurd to the young man who held the weight of such high expectations. Of course, being compared to Jordan, probably the greatest player in sports history, was an ego stroke, but... the folks drawing the comparison understood Jordan was a guard, right? Stackhouse, on the other hand, was not. In high school, he was a power forward, and he was a power forward at North Carolina. He'd never played guard before, had never pursued smaller players around and through screens, and had never come off screens for jump shots or drives. He could handle the ball a little, but the majority of his game was based on posting up, on having the ball in his hands with his back to the basket, and he had a long way to go to understand the nuances and develop the skills that would allow him to thrive as a guard... which is where the Sixers intended to play him.

Based on his experience, Stackhouse went into a situation for which he was not fully prepared once he joined the Sixers and the Philly pickup circuit, and that backdrop is crucial to sorting and separating truth from fabrication or exaggeration in the stories of that summer. Because he was so young and turned out to be so great, there's a natural tendency to elevate or exaggerate his feats in the Fieldhouse and at the Bellevue and at the other gyms that he and the Sixers and other Philly pro and college players frequented, because the exaggeration amplifies his legend. Everyone who tells a story about Kobe's involvement in those games interprets those memories through their own interests and perspectives. John Lucas believed he had discovered a hidden gem. Assuming he would still be the Sixers' coach and general manager in June 1996, he had already decided to choose Kobe. He only told this strategy to the individuals he trusted the most in basketball, and there is a powerful, renowned legacy in being the coach who saw Kobe coming before anyone else. Mo Howard was practically Lucas and Joe Bryant's brother. Jerry Stackhouse has had to listen to these anecdotes for the past two decades, and each one pricks his ego, because implicit in each one is a dig on him, his profession, and his ability: Kobe taught you one-on-one. Kobe dominated you. Kobe wasn't even a high school senior yet, and he was destroying the third pick in the draft, which was you. And so ...

Willie Burton, a journeyman NBA guard, had previously played for the Sixers in 1994-95. In December, he set the Spectrum's single-game scoring record with 53 points against the Miami Heat, and he justified his astounding one-off performance with two words: "Just hoopin'." He arrived at St. Joe's, played a game, and had to guard Kobe. Burton scored the first time he touched the ball and then yelled at Kobe. Kobe scored ten of his team's eleven baskets the rest of the way. Burton only had one point. He stormed out of the Fieldhouse in a rage. He never returned to the gym or, for a year, the NBA. He signed with an Italian team and played there for the 1995-96 season. And so ...

Lucas would team Kobe against specific players for one-on-one games after the Sixers practised. Vernon Maxwell, who had just finished his seventh NBA season and was appropriately nicknamed "Mad Max," was once his partner/adversary. The league had suspended him for ten games in February for storming into the stands and assaulting a supporter who was berating and heckling him.

"They were playing to ten," Lucas explained, "and it got down to nine-nine." It was so rough that I believed they were going to fight. 'I want somebody who's going to fight at nine-nine,' I told myself. And so ...

Bobby Johnson, who attended Southern High School in Philadelphia and was the sixth man on La Salle's three consecutive conference championship teams in the 1980s, would often accompany his former teammate Lionel "L-Train" Simmons to the St. Joe's runs. For a game versus five Sixers, Simmons and Johnson of the Sacramento Kings teamed up with Kobe, former Sixers centre Rick Mahorn, and Philly native and former NBA guard Paul "Snoop" Graham. The first person to ten won.

"The score is tied at nine; we have the ball," remarked Johnson. "Kobe brings the ball up, which Vernon Maxwell on the right wing defends. Here comes Kobe, banging the ball and instructing NBA veterans to clear the court. Train was the first to post up, and he cleared him out of the thread, followed by Snoop. Mahorn waved off the screen. I had no need to take my butt anywhere near him after viewing this."

Kobe dribbled between his legs, crossed Maxwell over, and took a sixteen-foot jump shot against Maxwell. "Dagger over Maxwell," said Johnson. "He said 'Ballgame' as if he'd been there before. "I was astounded beyond belief." And so ...

Kobe faced Sixers forward Sharone Wright, the sixth overall pick in the 1994 draft, in a game of P-I-G. A chance to ride about in Wright's Land Cruiser is at risk. "I concentrated really hard, and I beat him," remarked Kobe once. "I was supposed to be gone for five or ten minutes, but instead I drove around for half an hour." And so …

Howard was present at every workout. During one game, Kobe took off from the foul line and attempted to dunk over the Sixers' seven-foot-six centre, Shawn Bradley. He didn't make it. "But none of the professional guys were doing that," Howard pointed out. "There was no anxiety. There was no uncertainty. There was alpha, alpha, and alpha again. You'd think he'd defer because these people were older than him. But his catchphrase was always, 'I'm going to be the best player on the floor this session.'" On a morning when the Fieldhouse was closed, the players and coaches, including Lucas' assistant Maurice Cheeks, went across City Avenue to the gym at Episcopal Academy. Stackhouse and Kobe stood guard over each other. "Jerry is a pretty good player," Howard said, "but Kobe is giving him a run for his money." I'll never forget one particular play. Kobe is guarding Jerry and protecting him fiercely, and Jerry became frustrated and hip-tossed Kobe. I swear to you, Kobe gets up and gets the ball, and he hits a thirty-foot shot. He understood what he was doing when he banked it. When Maurice looks at me, he says, 'If Jerry Stackhouse is No. 3, Kobe has to be 3A.'" And so …

Kobe picked up Emory Dabney one August morning and rolled up the windows and turned up the heat in the car on the way to St. Joe's.

"What exactly are you doing?" Dabney inquired. "I can't handle it anymore. It's 90 degrees outdoors."

"I'm about to play Stackhouse," Kobe announced. "I've got to stay warm." And so …

Jeremy Treatman was able to attend a few scrimmages and workouts, and Gregg Downer was also able to come because he had recently quit his phys-ed teaching job at The Shipley School and accepted one at Episcopal. On one play, Kobe took Treatman's breath away by driving into the lane, rising over Mahorn—six foot ten, 240 pounds, a former member of the "Bad Boy" Detroit Pistons capable of flattening Kobe with a forearm and happy to do so—and bending around Mahorn midair, his hand and the ball above the rim, for a layup. The most telling discovery of that July and August, according to Treatman, was that Bradley would occasionally bring Kobe home from workouts, then contact him each night to confirm that he would be there the next morning. That was interesting. That was important. That meant Kobe belonged, that he fit in, and in the grand scheme of things, belonging was everything. The Minnesota Timberwolves had recently selected Kevin Garnett with the fifth overall pick, making him the first player drafted out of high school in twenty years, and "that made Kobe want to do it even more," according to Treatman. "When he was growing up in Italy, college basketball wasn't as important to him as it was to everyone else." The NBA thoughts became more serious throughout those sessions." And so …

Lucas asked a couple of Episcopal players to join the workouts as warm bodies: set picks, throw passes in drills, nothing that the average high school player couldn't handle. Participating in the drills was a dream come true for Michael Weil, a sophomore on the JV team—six feet tall, 145 pounds, short blond hair, "pale as shit," he said—for a kid who had never been so close to a professional athlete before. But it was Kobe who got the majority of Weil's attention and interest. A high school senior... going full throttle against the Sixers... Weil was astounded. Weil sought and obtained Kobe's autograph out of all the athletes and prominent names present. He handed him a slip of notebook paper and asked, "What sports do you play?" Kobe was glad to sign it, was conversational and polite, and asked, "What sports do you play?" This boy is only two years older than I am, Weil thought, making what he saw each day after the scrimmages concluded all the more memorable.

"Kobe and Stack were going at it on one of the side hoops," Weil explained. I'm not sure what number they played, what the final score was, or anything else. But it didn't take a basketball analyst to notice that the two guys playing one-on-one on the side were nearly equal in ability." And so …

Stop. Simply put an end to it. Didn't everyone else in the gym notice what Jerry Stackhouse noticed? Doesn't everyone else who was there remember the same things he does? Didn't anyone else notice Lionel Simmons, former Temple stars Eddie Jones and Mark Macon, and all the old heads from Philly basketball yelling at Kobe to pass the ball?

So... pause. Yes, Kobe had some good scoring days due to his ability to move and handle the ball so efficiently, but his tunnel vision was absolute and all-encompassing. Nobody wanted to play alongside Kobe. Nobody would ever pick him for a pickup game. Oh, he defeated Stackhouse in a one-on-one match. Stackhouse was three and a half years Kobe's senior. "Could you imagine a seventeen-year-old beating me consistently?" According to Stackhouse. "I'd hurt him first." The truth. I was only physically ill—something like that could never happen to me. Did we compete one-on-one? Yes. Did he assault me? Did he possibly win a game? Yes. Did he consistently beat Jerry Stackhouse when he was twenty and he was seventeen? Hell. No. That's the end of that narrative. Was he exceptionally gifted, and did everyone see enormous potential in him? Yes. But when you talk to folks who were there in the gym, those moments that we hear in Kobe Bryant lore now have a somewhat different perspective."

Everyone at the 1995 Adidas ABCD Camp at Fairleigh Dickinson University would have known that Kobe Bryant was the best high school basketball player in the country because Kobe would have been the one telling everyone, posting on Twitter and Facebook, and sharing video of himself on Instagram. But, in July, the internet was still a mystery to the majority of Americans, a new technology whose full power and reach had yet to be revealed, allowing Sonny Vaccaro to keep his scheme to reclaim control of the athletic-shoe business covert. Vaccaro had not intended to tie Adidas' future to a high school superstar when he entered that summer, lacking Nike's financial resources and brand strength, and before Garnett went so high in the NBA. His job was to discover the next Michael Jordan, but the risk of signing a seventeen- or eighteen-year-old and putting him at the centre of the organisation's hopes for a comeback was too large. Perhaps the safer bet was Kerry Kittles, a long and supple shooting guard returning for his senior season at Villanova with a style of play comparable to Jordan's. "He would have probably been the guy I recommended to Adidas," Vaccaro recalls. "Kerry was a famous name, a legitimate athlete with a long career. He had nothing bad to say about himself. Kevin, on the other hand, unlocked the doors." And Vaccaro's mind was opened. He had this... type of... link... with Kobe Bryant and his family—with the father, Joe, a once-forgotten figure from the past, and with the boy, loaded with so many precious possibilities. Sonny Vaccaro did not believe in coincidences, and they had found each other after all these years, at this precise moment in time. Gregg Downer had found it easy, oh so easy, to goad Kobe in the years and months leading up to this ABCD Camp, to create the perfect method of motivation for a player who entered every gym believing, knowing in his bones, that there wasn't another player in the place better than him. It only needed a quick glance at a recruiting rating or a list in a basketball magazine for Downer to have enough information for ammunition. This week, who was ahead of Kobe? Vince Carter, are you a student at Mainland High School in Daytona Beach? What about Tim Thomas? Kobe became agitated at the mention of a name or two. Even in his final years, Kobe would bring up his former coaches mocking and its ability to encourage him. You used to tell me that Vince Carter or Tim Thomas were superior. It wasn't quite true—Downer was always careful to point out that those two were rated higher as recruits than Kobe, not that they were better than him—but it served its purpose for both of them.

When Downer, his older brother, Drew, and Mike Egan drove north to Hackensack for the camp, they quickly understood how ineffective it would be to compare Kobe to other exceptional high school players. Gregg had asked Drew to join his coaching staff for the 1995-96 season, and Drew, who was working and living in Orlando as an executive for a flooring firm at the time, agreed, resigning his career and leaving the sun behind for the chance to train Kobe. Gregg trusted Drew to be an emotional barometer for the team, to pick up on whether guys needed a pat on the back or an angry talking-to if they weren't prepared for the pressure on him, Kobe, and the Aces to win a state championship. Drew, for his part, realised straight away that Kobe was probably the least of his worries in that regard. None of the other campers were pushing themselves as hard as he was. "I kept waiting for Kobe to let up on the gas," Drew recounted, "but he never did." In reality, it was clear from the start of camp that Kobe was overcompensating. "He played a game," Egan explained, "and he was... not goofing off, but looking to do more than he should have," striving too hard to be the best player on the floor, to wow the college coaches and pro scouts in the seats. After that, Egan approached him and asked, "Hey, man, what are you doing?" Simply play your game. Just keep doing what you're doing. "The next game he played—I'm not saying it was because of me—he did a move where he did a stop, a spin, and a fifteen-foot bank shot, and I just saw every coach's jaw drop," Egan recalled. "It was an unstoppable NBA-level move." Nobody, at any level, could ever stop a six-foot-six-inch youngster from shooting that shot. That is exactly what the coaches want to see. He was really breaking away from the pack there."

Mike Krzyzewski had surgery for a slipped disk in his back in October 1994, six months after Duke had fallen by four points to Arkansas in the NCAA championship game, but he was still in so much pain for months after the procedure that he believed the disk was the cause. He was concerned that, like his friend and former North Carolina State coach Jim Valvano, he would succumb to disease and die. All he needed was time and rest to allow the disk to recover properly, but the Blue Devils crumbled while he was away. In Krzyzewski's absence, longtime assistant Pete Gaudet coached, and Duke finished the '94-'95 season with a 13-18 record, the situation becoming so tense that former NBA coach Doug Collins, who had been Joe Bryant's teammate with the Sixers and whose son

Chris played for the Blue Devils, charged into the locker room after one loss, screaming at Gaudet for not utilising Krzyzewski's players properly. Duke failed to qualify for the NCAA tournament for the first time in thirty-six years. Krzyzewski recovered sufficiently to resume coaching in the fall of 1995, and he returned to a team in desperate need of a superstar to restore its former grandeur.

Krzyzewski had designated his top assistant coach, Tommy Amaker, to operate as the key conduit between the Duke program and Kobe, having identified him as that superstar. Mike Egan was Amaker's main point of contact at Lower Merion. Amaker believed Kobe possessed all of the basketball and non-basketball traits that Duke sought in a player. His intelligence, breadth of perspective, and appreciation for diverse people and cultures that his years in Italy had produced were all layers to him. However, Amaker certainly spent more time discussing Kobe's probable future at Duke with Egan than Egan did with Kobe. "Kobe was very private about this stuff," Egan explained, "and we were very respectful of the fact that it was his decision and really not our business." 'Hey, let us know if you ever want to talk about it.' He did, however, have a remarkable capacity to compartmentalise things. We practically never discussed it with him."

Kobe, on the other hand, was on the phone with Krzyzewski, and he liked him right away. When they chatted early in the recruitment process, they discussed Kobe's experiences abroad and in his first few years back in the United States more than basketball. Krzyzewski had loved the way he had nurtured Grant Hill throughout Hill's four years at Duke, and Krzyzewski would tell Kobe stories and anecdotes about Hill: his taking over team leadership, his adapting to the media attention that the Blue Devils received. Hill had just ended his first season with the Detroit Pistons, who had taken him with the third overall choice in the 1994 draft, and had averaged nearly twenty points per game for them, earning a spot on the Eastern Conference all-star team and the NBA's Rookie of the Year Award. Kobe imagined Krzyzewski having the same effect on him. Late in his senior year, he would concede to those close to him what he was beginning to accept to himself: if he had to choose a college, he would go to Duke without a doubt. Nobody knew that at the ABCD Camp: not Krzyzewski, not Speedy Morris, not Rick Pitino, not Syracuse's Jim Boeheim, whose leading scorer, guard Lawrence Moten, had just been selected in the second round of the NBA draft, and not Connecticut's Jim Calhoun and his sharp New England accent, who boasted to Kobe about his career win-loss record and UConn's back-to-back Big East championships. Every coach in the camp had the opportunity to sell Kobe on himself and his program, and every coach felt compelled to do so because no one knew what Kobe's plans were. So, as Gregg Downer and Egan boarded an elevator inside the Rothman Center, Krzyzewski snuck in as well. It was the first time he and Downer had actually met. Krzyzewski may now physically make his elevator pitch to Kobe's head coach.

We polish diamonds at Duke, he said to Downer. We know they're fantastic, and we're going to improve them. That's a terrific line, Egan thought. Kobe fulfilled a promise he made to Sonny Vaccaro a year earlier at a camp with Rip Hamilton, Lester Earl, Shaheen Holloway, and Jermaine O'Neal, while that "Fab Five" was still talking about joining forces at La Salle. He was selected the camp's most valuable player, therefore making him the top high school athlete in the country. Joe basked in the attention lavished on his son at the coronation. Coaches' phone calls had been flooding the Bryants' house, disrupting the family's meals; it wasn't like that for him while he was at Bartram, but he relished it on Kobe's behalf. "You wouldn't believe how many people have told me how much they enjoy watching him play," Joe said at the camp. What about Kobe's college selection? "I'm trying to steer away from college right now," Joe explained. "Kobe will have plenty of time to choose a college." The key thing now is to drink it all in because this is a once-in-a-lifetime opportunity." Besides, news had spread. Everyone knew, or would know, who would be at the top of those recruitment rankings from that point on. Everyone knew, or was about to learn, who the king was. Vaccaro had soon sent Kerry Kittles to the depths of his imagination. He decided that Kobe was the player that matched the scale of his desire for Adidas. This would have to be done perfectly, with the proper agency and partner for Kobe. Who had a similar Philadelphia background to the Bryants. Who, like Vaccaro, believed that an aspiring professional athlete had the right to pursue his or her career as he or she saw fit, and that college should not be required for a player to reach the NBA. Who would share Vaccaro's vision of Kobe becoming basketball's next godchild, and who had the clout to pull the strings and make it happen? Vaccaro called Arn Tellem later that summer. Krzyzewski planned for a trip to suburban Philadelphia to see one of Kobe's games in the Plymouth Whitemarsh summer league. He made a wise choice in going up against Donnie Carr and Roman Catholic. It wasn't often that a summer-league showdown prompted gamesmanship 24 hours before tip-off, but...... Carr was conversing on his house phone with his girlfriend the night before the game when the call-waiting beeped. He moved his mouse over.

"Hello."

"Yo, Don. What's up, dude? "What exactly is going on?"

"Chillin'. "Who is this?"

"Man, Bean. "How are you doing?"

"I'm chillin', man. "I'm talking to my girl."

"All right, dude. I just wanted to ask you a short inquiry. "Will Yah Davis be at the game tomorrow?"

Davis, Carr's Roman teammate and a Division I prospect, was said to be transferring to Frankford High School. Carr's antennae immediately tense. This guy is out fishing. This wasn't the same kind of inquiry Kobe used to ask him when they were younger, when he

47

questioned him about life in South Philly, about growing up without the suburban pleasures Kobe had, about saving money just to splurge once in a while at a fast-food restaurant. This was not the result of genuine interest. This was a gentle question. This was a contender looking for an advantage over his opponent.

"I don't know," Carr admitted. "Why?"

"Man," Kobe responded, "if Yah comes to the game, it'll be you and Yah against me, and we'll get it on." That would be a great matchup between you and Yah. But if it's just you, man, I'm not sure it's worth my time to come."

Carr grabbed the phone above his head and slammed it down on the receiver, oblivious to the fact that his girlfriend was still on the other end of the line. His sister and brother entered the room: What's the matter? We were awakened by a loud noise. Carr couldn't believe Kobe had the balls to pick up the phone, dial that number, and play mind games with him. Carr and his pals used to tease and push this scrawny little joker around the court.

"Man, this motherfucker just called me!" Carr yelled at his siblings. "Total disrespect!"

The next day at Plymouth Whitemarsh, John Lucas, Rick Pitino, and Krzyzewski sat among the twenty or so people sweltering in the gym's thick, heavy air. One of Kobe's teammates, Dave Rosenberg, looked up at them. Oh my god, he thought, this season is going to be intense. Mike Egan was relieved that Krzyzewski had made it to the game at all. Egan, Lower Merion's head coach in that league, had given him instructions to the gym, concerned that the famed coach would end up in Allentown rather than Montgomery County. Faced with such a plethora of coaches, Carr sought an assistant on Roman's staff. "I want to guard Kobe," Carr explained. "I want to show Kobe and everybody else that I'm better." They didn't shake hands or speak to each other as they walked onto the court for tip-off, and when a Roman player batted the ball to Carr, Kobe dropped into "a big-time defensive stance," Carr recalled, "like when Jordan was guarding Magic in the Finals," arms and legs extended and wide, like a giant spider. Yes, I recall what you used to do to me. But now it's a novelty. Carr came at Kobe at a quick pace and slid to the basket. Kobe came up to him at the rim, pulled off from behind him to try to block his shot, but no... Carr duped him by dishing to a trailing teammate for a power slam. The first half finished with him having 25 points and Kobe having four. Carr laughed quietly to himself. He knew he could score on Kobe at any time. "If I went side to side with him, going north and south with some shifty moves," Carr explained, "he'd have a hard time staying in front of me because his lateral quickness wasn't as good as it had become." Nothing was different from those Sonny Hill League games, when Carr could move Kobe around like a chess piece, moving him just about anywhere he wanted thanks to his size and strength advantage.

Then the second half began, and for the first time, everything was different between them. On defence, Kobe began face-guarding Carr, denying him the ball, and when Carr did get it, Kobe sank his shoulders, refusing to allow Carr get beneath him. On one of Roman's possessions, the point guard attempted to force a pass to Carr. Kobe took it, tipped it ahead of himself, and chased it down. A Roman player rushed in on the ball, but Kobe snatched it, whipped it behind his back and in front of him again, and continued to drive for the hoop. Two more Roman players approached Kobe, who threw the ball between his legs, from behind his buttocks to in front of his crotch, an outlet throw to himself. He retrieved the bouncing ball one step inside the foul line at full speed, soared, and dunked it with two hands—BOOM—and when he landed, he began shouting. "It was pure elation," Carr added. "He gave that look that said, 'I'm the best player on the floor, and don't forget it.'"

Egan was honoured to get the note, but no matter how much he wished he knew what Kobe's conclusion would be, he didn't. Today, he keeps the letter hanging in the centre of a wall in his home office in Paoli, Pennsylvania, across from a bookcase brimming with autobiographies and massive historical histories, rather than in a desk drawer or buried somewhere out of sight. A Duke basketball, striped blue and white with a Blue Devils head logo, rested atop a desk at Joe Bryant's old study at 1224 Remington Road, just fourteen miles distant, on an early September day in 2020. The couple that lived there, Richard and Kate Bayer, had no idea why Kobe had left it behind, but they, like everyone else, could speculate.

It didn't take long for the Sixers' potential saviour to realise the deck was stacked against him. Joe Carbone, the team's strength and conditioning coach, was watching a long, lanky boy stroll into the Fieldhouse and head right to Lucas on July 31, 1995, a month after the team had picked Stackhouse. After a brief private conversation, Lucas summoned Carbone and presented him to Kobe. Carbone, a former professional bodybuilder who had spent his entire life living and working in Rockland County, New York, until joining the Sixers that season, was stocky, muscled, and built like a fire hydrant. He knew nothing about the high school basketball culture in Philadelphia and had no idea who Kobe was, and at five feet two, he looked up at the six-foot-six youngster. You need to get with Joe and grow stronger, Lucas said Kobe. The remodelling of Kobe Bryant's body began right away, with Carbone guiding Kobe over to a haphazard pile of training equipment and gear in the gym's corner. There was no dedicated weight room at the Fieldhouse, only a squat rack with two benches, a couple of selectorized and pin-loaded machines, and some high-low pulleys and cables. "But you can get around that if you know what you're doing," Carbone remarked. You can perform all of the lifts." Because the Sixers and other players began their workouts at 9:00 a.m., Kobe and Carbone began theirs at 7:00 a.m., and they would continue in full view of all the other athletes. Carbone later admitted that the arrangement was awkward because it was evident who the true chosen one was.

To keep track of Kobe's training and improvement, Carbone constructed a spreadsheet. He's kept it ever since, so he can show you that Kobe's first weight-training session with him included four rounds of exercises, ranging from back-squatting 65 pounds for ten repetitions to three sets of twenty curl-ups to push-pressing 105 pounds for ten repetitions. By the third session, on Thursday, August 3, Kobe was closing with ten 135-pound back-squat reps. "He was built to be an endurance guy," stated Carbone. "His muscles were built to last. He wasn't a quick twitch. Fast-twitch muscles allow you to sprint quickly and build massive, dense muscles. You see an NFL running back with strong thighs who can bench 400 pounds and squat 600 pounds. Because that wasn't Kobe's body type, his gains were difficult. They did not come cheap. But he did benefit." By the conclusion of the summer, Kobe had increased his weight from 185 to 200 pounds, the fifteen extra pounds consisting of muscle and sinew. Phil Martelli would catch him cycling on an exercise bike or sprinting with a parachute connected to his torso, Carbone nearby watching him. This is unlike anything else I've seen from all these previous great athletes passing through Philadelphia, Martelli thought. "He was there to prepare," Martelli subsequently explained, "not to play."

John Nash, the general manager of the Washington Bullets, was a Philly Guy—an alumnus of St. Joseph's University, once a longtime official with the Sixers, an insider who knew where all the bodies were buried, a man for whom a handshake was a bond. "If John says something," Frank Layden, the Utah Jazz's long-time president and coach, reportedly observed, "you can put it in the bank." Nash and Joe Bryant had a cordial relationship while Nash was the director of the Philadelphia Big Five in the mid-1970s. They moved in the same circles, and Nash was familiar with the Bryants and their reputation as a stable, grounded family.

I love keeping secrets, in case you haven't noticed that by now.

—KOBE BRYANT

CHAPTER 4

SECRETS AND SHARKS

Before his last season of Lower Merion basketball began, Kobe Bryant would wake up to the darkness and stillness of a predawn morning in late October, wrap himself into the driver's seat of his Land Cruiser, and embark on a two-mile ride to his high school. Nothing would be open yet, including groceries and bagel businesses. Nobody would be on the street or the sidewalks for a while. If he slept a few more minutes, if he slipped out the front door a little later, he'd pass another car or see a jogger or two in his peripheral vision, steady as metronomes, breath steaming the ten inches in front of their faces, the streetlights' soft glow glinting off their reflective vests. There wouldn't be anything to distract him when he exited the driveway, turned right onto Haverford Avenue, and then right again into Argyle Road. There, for all the densely packed houses and the go-go-go lifestyles of the baby boomers who live in those houses, all would be silent, with only porch lights or the glare of a full moon puncturing the canopy of darkness.

The speed limit on any street on his route would not exceed 35 mph, thus the trip would take him around seven minutes. Perhaps it would take less than seven minutes since he was a teenager who was impatient and wanted to get to school as soon as possible, so his foot would give the gas pedal a greater push, and the SUV would reach speeds of 40 to 45 mph. Perhaps it would take him longer than seven minutes since he was a Black adolescent driving about the Main Line and would want to be cautious because one never knows where a cop might be and what that cop might think when he sees a Black youngster driving around the Main Line in the predawn darkness.

His windows were closed and his heat was turned on, so the silence was complete at times. Would he visualise and plan out the morning's exercise, including foot drills, three-pointers, and midrange shots? Would he be thinking about his team's upcoming practice or game? Would he picture himself in the NBA, with the fans roaring and the game-winning shot at his disposal? He wouldn't always drive alone. He would occasionally stop by Robby Schwartz's house to pick him up. Schwartz, a stumpy junior guard, was one of the team's most likeable players, a burbling fizz of one-liners and amusing anecdotes. He'd spent the two days of tryouts running around the gym, diving for every loose ball, taking every charge, and winning every sprint. "I've never practised so hard in my life," he subsequently said. "I had no choice but to join the team." I knew something extraordinary was about to occur, and I wanted to be a part of it."

Kobe would park in the faculty lot, near an access to one of the school's three gymnasiums, an act of entitlement that some may argue he should not have been granted. Construction at and around the school that fall had reduced the number of student-allocated parking spaces from 79 to 24, and because residents were so irritated by the cars clogging their sweetgum-shaded neighbourhoods, police were issuing forty-dollar tickets to students who dared to park on the streets near campus. And Kobe can park his SUV wherever he wants, as if he's the principal? But he could easily defend himself, weave the justification. He was getting to school before 5:30 a.m., before any faculty or students, and if he was spending more time in that building honing his craft than they were, if he was destined for fame and immortality—and he was certain he was—why were they more deserving of one of those parking spots than he was? So a janitor would let Kobe into the school, and he and Schwartz would enter either the main gym or the school's tertiary facility, known as "the Ardmore Gym." In any case, it would take five minutes for the lights to turn on and a half hour for the gym to warm up to room temperature, and as Schwartz stood there, shivering in his shorts—"I have never been so cold as I was in that gym"—he wondered why, when Kobe had asked several teammates if they wanted to join him for these shootarounds, he had been the one to say, Sure.

A high school exhibits unrivalled confidence and self-assurance at that point in his or her life. A high school senior has the run of the school for the first semester and can coast through the second, once college applications have been submitted and acceptance letters are filling his or her mailbox, once he or she has a better sense of what's ahead, once summer—his or her first as a high school graduate, as an eighteen-year-old, as an adult—and its new freedom are in sight. A high school senior knows the terrain of his or her daily existence, what's cool and what isn't. A high school senior receives the bigger locker, the best table in the lunch, and party invitations. A senior in high school struts.

Kobe Bryant had more reason to strut than most high school seniors. All traces of that shy, inexperienced freshman were gone, replaced by a seventeen-year-old who had shown to himself that his dream of playing in the NBA was not only achievable, but also within reach. That understanding set him free. He was always aware of his place, function, and duties in the Lower Merion environment. But he was also willing and eager to test limits, both others' and his own, within and outside of school, trying on moods, images, and identities as if they were department store outfits. When a homeless man approached him and Matt Matkov on a Philadelphia street and asked for money, Kobe grabbed him up and hurled him away. Matkov got into a brawl at the Shack in Ardmore, and after Kobe intervened and defused the situation, he warned Matkov, "Matt, you can't be making n——s mad like that." You simply cannot." When a restaurant server brought him a small piece of apple pie one night, he told her, "Ma'am, I'm six-six." This isn't going to fill me up." His goal to become the finest basketball player in the world consumed him so much that his buddies didn't realise the impact it had on him until he was gone.

It was one of Kobe's defining paradoxes throughout his life. He could sympathise, and he couldn't. He shared a room with Jordan Couzens, the ice hockey club's star, and Kobe frequently drove out to King of Prussia to watch games and cheer him on. "I think Kobe recognized he got all the attention," a classmate said, "but Jordan still owns every record at Lower Merion for ice hockey, and there was a kinship between the two of them." Matkov found a way to redirect the topic back to Kobe during an English class examination of Flannery O'Connor's short tale "Everything That Rises Must Converge," arguing that the narrative's main character had deluded himself, had failed to be honest with himself, in a way that Kobe would never do. "A lot of people think he's living in a bubble, his own world," Matkov continued, his ponytail bobbing as he talked and nodded at Kobe, "but I know he's not." He's linked to me, and he's linked to himself. It doesn't get any more genuine than him." To be in the classroom at that time was to be torn between admiring Matkov for his devotion to his hero/best mate and rolling your eyes at his sycophancy. Kobe was teamed with his buddy Lauren Rodrick for a home-economics project, which he met when she transferred to Lower Merion as a junior after attending Catholic school for six years. She'd told him how awkward she felt as a new student, and he'd said he understood. Their home-ec instructor had given them a Cabbage Patch doll for the time-honoured practice of high school students learning what it's like to be parents, caring for a newborn. Rodrick, who has fair skin, burst out laughing when Kobe looked at the doll's darker tone and questioned, "Are you sure this is your baby?" She regarded him to be witty, a jokester who was more at ease in one-on-one circumstances than in groups. Rodrick saw that the larger they gathered around Kobe, the quieter he became. She had been startled when he informed her when they were juniors that, while he had obviously been out with two or three pals at a time, he had never been to a house party, never been among a couple of dozen high school kids without his or anyone else's parents overseeing. "Kobe, you might be going off to college," Rodrick had said. "You can't possibly go without going to a house party!" So, after attempting to deflect Rodrick's insistence—"Naw, I'm gonna stay home, and you guys go have fun," Kobe had accompanied her, her boyfriend, Shaya, and a few others to a house in Yeadon, a small city in Delaware County, and let the music and attention from girls he had never met before take him away for one Saturday night. "He was a hot commodity," Rodrick said. "He was so guarded about life, but he was enjoying the girls not knowing who he was because he was Kobe Bryant." He was just a handsome man at a party. It had been a very good night. He was grateful that he went."

At Lower Merion, he no longer had that freedom and relative obscurity. On October 3, students turned their attention to the screens in the halls and lobby for the end of the O. J. Simpson murder trial, and the not-guilty judgement divided the school, with black students rejoicing and white students in disbelief, but the tension never reached Kobe. "I don't know how much people saw him as black or white as much as they saw him as Kobe, this looming figure," Schwartz explained. "He was among us, but he was bigger than us in some ways." He was becoming more at ease with his elevated social standing, as well as with himself. On weekends, he and Griffin went out more regularly, to clubs and other locations in and around the city. A story spread around the school that he had started dating actress Tatyana Ali, who appeared in the comedy The Fresh Prince of Bel-Air, a rumour that Kobe himself had initiated by joking with his buddy Rennae Williams that he would take Ali or pop star/actor Brandy to the senior prom. (When Melanie Amato, a Merionite reporter, questioned if the rumour was genuine, he laughed. "No comment," he said.) Because of his standing, he made an effect on everyone in the building in every interaction. Frank Hartwell, his guidance counsellor, was talking with some freshmen when Kobe rushed into Hartwell's office and interfered. "Hi, Mr. Hartwell," he said. "How's it going with your family?" The freshman exclaimed, then stared at him. Here comes Kobe Bryant! I'm right next to him!

Gregg Downer had been feeling the strain of coaching Kobe and seeking a state championship even before trials and practices began in late autumn 1995. He expected that this would be his final season at Lower Merion. He had accepted his new job as a phys-ed teacher at Episcopal Academy with two understandings: first, that he would have the opportunity to coach the Aces for Kobe's entire senior season; second, that once the season was over, he would devote himself fully to teaching and coaching at Episcopal, even if he never became the school's head basketball coach. But what if there was no district or state championship? What if the season was a flop in some way? The daily challenge of Kobe, of pushing and being pushed by him, was energising, but Downer couldn't put an end to the questioning. Downer used to lie awake at night before Kobe arrived in Lower Merion, afraid not that the Aces wouldn't win their next game, but that they wouldn't score. It seemed ridiculous, yet it was true. Now, if he wasn't cautious, the tension could cripple him, and others were feeling it as well. Kobe participated in a seniors-vs.-juniors tug-of-war at a football pep rally, with five kids on one side and five on the other, upperclassmen supremacy on the line. When Lynne Freeland, the teacher who organised the pep rally and the mother of Kobe's friend Susan Freeland, saw how close Kobe was to stepping on the bags, she scrambled to kick and heave them out of the way. Gregg will kill me if Kobe strains his ankle, she thought. The phone never stopped ringing in the athletic office—a broom closet-sized space barely big enough to hold the director, Tom McGovern, and the secretary, Mary Murray—coaches, scouts, reporters, parents, and community members. McGovern purchased an answering machine that could carry up to a hundred messages. He disconnected it after two days of turning on the lights in the office and finding the machine full since the calls had continued to come in overnight. Throughout the regular season, there would be so many requests for tickets, and the lines to buy them would be so long, that McGovern had to shift ticket sales out of the sports office since the office was in an academic area, and the lines were interrupting hallway traffic during school hours. On game evenings, hundreds of people who thought they could buy tickets right before kickoff were turned away at the entrance, causing traffic jams along Montgomery Avenue and headaches for the township police. "By his junior and senior years," McGovern recalled, "Kobe had occupied almost every minute of my day." Murray's, too, though she wasn't as upbeat about it. She seemed to be the person at Lower Merion who detested or disapproved of The Kobe Experience the most, as if having a terrible basketball program was preferable to the hustle and excitement inside the school and the emphasis on it. "They were getting overwhelmed," said Downer. "Someone like Mary Murray was looking forward to the season's end."

Despite the pressure, Downer and the rest of the team couldn't wait for the season to begin. The Aces, while still Kobe-centric, would have a different look without Guy Stewart and Evan Monsky, who had both graduated. Emory Dabney would take over as point guard, joining Kobe, Jermaine Griffin, Dan Pangrazio, and Brendan Pettit in the starting lineup, and two more new players, forward Omar Hatcher, who had transferred from Archbishop Carroll, and freshman Kareem Barksdale, gave Downer a deeper bench. Downer packed the Aces' early-season schedule, as he had done the year before: a game against Donnie Carr and Roman Catholic at Drexel University; a rematch with St. Anthony, this time at the Fieldhouse at St. Joseph's; and three games at the Beach Ball Classic, a tournament in Myrtle Beach, South Carolina, that would feature several of the nation's best players and teams, including Glen Oaks and Lester Earl, Eau Claire (South Carolina) and

Most importantly, for the sake of the squad and his personal peace of mind, Downer hired two more assistant coaches and assigned them odd tasks. He didn't have to seek out the first coach; the first coach sought him out. Jimmy Kieserman, who was six feet tall and twenty-six years old, had grown up with Sam Rines Jr. and had started at point guard for both Rider University and the University of Miami, and who was now working in insurance and living in Narberth, happened to see a feature about Kobe on a local TV news station one night. Kieserman, the grandson of famous Temple head coach Harry Litwack, asked himself a question that any good coach, or the grandson of a great one, would ask: How is this kid doing in high school? Who is on hand to assist him? He phoned Downer and offered to be a sort of trainer for Kobe. Kieserman has the ability to dunk. Kieserman had competed in the Maccabi Games in Israel and professionally in the Eastern Basketball League, and he had developed an athletic, aggressive game. "I felt like a man, and he was a kid, and I could help him with his skill set, push him around," he explained. Downer agreed. Downer's second hire, Jeremy Treatman, was a formality because the two men were already friends and Treatman spent so much time with Downer, Kobe, and Joe. Downer informed Treatment that he would be more of a public relations director than a coach. Downer despised the constant interview requests from press and television reporters most of all the obligations that came with having Kobe on the team. Downer preferred to focus on coaching his team, and not only did Treatman have the professional contacts, experience, and know-how to handle the media onslaught, but he was ecstatic about the chance to be an intimate to Kobe and to abandon any pretence of objectivity when it came to his relationships within the program. Why should he cover Lower Merion basketball when he could be a part of it? To Downer's credit, it was a creative and modern approach to assembling a high school basketball coaching staff. Mike Egan would continue to be the defensive specialist. The amateur sports psychologist would be Drew Downer. Downer would oversee and coordinate the entire operation, with Kieserman acting as Kobe's foil/tutor.

The road would not be without difficulties in the early weeks of the season. Egan's preseason notes, titled "4 Months to Play, a Lifetime to Regret," left little question that the tough-love methods adopted by Downer and him during Kobe's junior season would be carried over to his senior season: "Kobe—stronger in the paint, rebounds, modifying, patrolling... Jermaine—finish, finish, finish, finish, finish, finish, finish, 2nd effort... DAN—court awareness, more ball handling, pump + go. Consider agility work for him (heavy feet)." They would do everything they could to treat Kobe as if he were simply another member of the squad, even though he clearly wasn't. On the first day of practice, Kobe was astounded by his teammates' sloth, particularly those who were new to him. Dabney was late and would be academically ineligible for three games because he was "just fucking around and not doing my work," as he put it. Hatcher and another backup, Cary "Butter" Walker, were also late. "They had no idea," Kobe subsequently said. "They tried out for the basketball team but were unsure what to expect. They had no idea what we were about to go through emotionally, the hype, and the media. They had no idea. They were just doggin it at practice." He took Griffin, his closest teammate, aside.

Before a single game that season, Kobe's skills and fervent desire to win were separating him from his teammates, who were struggling to live up to his expectations for them. Downer had the squad do a rebounding drill every practice: one player chased the wayward shot, while the other tried to box him out. The defender had to stay on the court if the offensive player ever touched the ball, let alone grabbed the rebound. During his high school career, Kobe had never lost a scrimmage or competitive drill. So, when he and Pangrazio were pitted against one other and chased a loose ball against a concrete wall, Kobe did what he felt was necessary. Kobe slammed Pangrazio in the small of his back just as he got his hands on the basketball. At the bottom of the wall, a metal plate hung. As Pangrazio collided with the pavement, his elbow collided with one of the plate's fasteners, severing his arm. Kobe snatched the ball from Pangrazios bloodied hands and brought it to centre court, delighted that he had remained unbeaten. Despite the fact that he immediately went to the hospital to have three stitches threaded into his arm, Pangrazio showed no resentment for the incident. "As much as people might think Kobe went overboard," he later said, "we all loved his competitiveness." We were aware that we were a part of something remarkable. Kobe pushed me to levels I never believed possible and expected us all to do the same for him."

Robby Schwartz was a popular target for agony in general. Those morning carpools got him nowhere with Kobe. When the Aces scrimmaged full-court, Downer frequently had them play six-on-five, with Schwartz and another small player, Leo Stacy, guarding and irritating Kobe. "I would always think to myself, 'One of these times, he's going to haul off and hit me,'" Schwartz remembered. "We had a crush on him. We'd try not to give him the ball, but if he did, we'd double-team him, hack him, and foul him. It became a little dicey at points. He was going to smack our hand away. "I got hit in the face with the ball several times after a dunk." Schwartz finally got his revenge once, driving towards Kobe on a fast break and spinning the ball off the backboard for a layup. When Kobe flopped to the floor, Schwartz caught the ball as it slid through the basket and threw it at him while he was still down on his back. Yes, absolutely. I just scored on the country's best player. When he saw his teammates pointing at him, Schwartz went back on defence, pumping his hands as he approached half-court. "I turned around," he explained, "and the ball was coming straight at my face." Kobe had thrown it at him in the Nolan Ryan fashion. Schwartz took a step back. The ball flew by his head. The practice session continued as if nothing had happened.

But there was one incident with Schwartz that has long been woven into the tapestry of the Kobe Bryant story, though the details have blurred over time and retellings to the point that the anecdote might as well be legend. According to people who witnessed the incident, the following is the most accurate account of what happened: The Aces were doing an intrasquad scrimmage at the time, and Kobe and Schwartz were on the same team. With the score deadlocked and Kobe consistently drawing double- and triple-teams, Schwartz came up with the brilliant idea of using Kobe as a decoy. Kobe slapped his hands and yelled for the ball in the corner—"Rob! Rob!"—but Schwartz faked a pass to him and drove to the hoop instead. It was his first shot of the game. "I missed the layup," Schwartz said. "I would tell you I got fouled, but we weren't really calling fouls." The opposing team scored to win the scrimmage, which was Kobe's first loss against his colleagues in four years. He smacked the ball to the ground. He chastised Schwartz, saying, "That wasn't the smart play!" What do you think you're doing? "It started off as playful and joking," Downer explained. "Then we realised,'He's not kidding.'" His rage grew to the point where Schwartz mumbled, "Dude, relax."

Time then came to a halt for Schwartz. Oh, shit, I should have kept my mouth shut. Kobe made a motion toward him, and Schwartz didn't linger to see what it was. He sprinted through the gym's double doors and ran to the top of the corridor. "I was terrified," he said. "I knew I'd said something to someone far bigger than myself. Fear seized over and I simply fled. Walking back into the gym... talk about humiliating."

Since then, whether Kobe "chased" Schwartz down the corridor has become legend. "He didn't chase after him," Egan explained. "The true tale is better: He was enraged at the guy. It made no difference that Robby was the final man on the bench." Treatman insisted that Kobe never took his gaze away from Schwartz for the remaining 75 minutes of practice, and as Treatman drove home that night, he couldn't get over what he'd seen, the intensity of Kobe's reaction to what anyone else would regard as a meaningless loss in just another scrimmage. He came to a stop at a traffic signal and realised the significance of the scene. That is what distinguishes him. That is what distinguishes him from everyone else.

"I think some of the kids were a little intimidated," said Treatman.

If Kobe's teammates couldn't manage his aggressiveness, how could they handle Roman Catholic? What about St. Anthony? Or, Chester, what about the district and state playoffs? Or, suppose the opposite scenario arose, and the other players became overconfident because they trusted Kobe to bail them out? Downer spotted hazards everywhere, including one caused by the team's assumed improvement. The Aces' general rise in talent had put Matt Matkov's roster status in jeopardy, and Downer worried about Kobe's reaction if the coaches couldn't keep Matkov on the team in good conscience.

"What am I going to do with this guy?" Downer inquired of Egan. "He can't really play for us, but he's Kobe's best friend."

"Cut him," Egan said. "Kobe won't notice for at least two weeks."

Matkov, as it turned out, quit the squad before Downer could fire him. Kobe looked around practice two weeks later and questioned, "What happened to Matkov?"

Joe Bryant had repeatedly told Speedy Morris over the past two years, "If Kobe goes to college, he'll go to La Salle." It was an easy thing for Joe to say to appease his boss and keep his job, but nothing had been resolved, and nothing would be, as far as Kobe and Joe were concerned. Morris and Joe's relationship had suffered a schism, which Morris was unaware of. Joe continued to communicate with Jeremy Treatman once a week, whispering into his office phone so Morris wouldn't hear, and updated Treatman on every conversation with Sonny Vaccaro. Joe, who was trying to balance being a parent and a recruiter, disliked the tone of Morris's queries about Kobe. "He was asking me as a recruiter," Joe once explained, "and I didn't appreciate that." On October 5, 1995, the Philadelphia Daily News published a report titled, "La Salle, NBA top Kobe Bryant's list," and Kobe snickered with derision at the headline. He'd told Pam, "Mom, there's no way I'm going to La Salle, no way in hell," and Joe, "Dad, it's not on you." Coach Morris is someone I despise."

Schwartz's time then came to a standstill. Oh my goodness, I should have kept my lips shut. Schwartz didn't linger to observe what Kobe was gesticulating at him. He dashed through the double doors of the gym and up the corridor. "I was terrified," he said. "I realised I'd said something to someone far larger than myself. Fear took hold of me, and I simply fled. Talk about humiliation walking back into the gym." Whether Kobe "chased" Schwartz down the corridor has now become legend. "He didn't chase after him," Egan said. "The truth is better: He was furious at the guy. It didn't matter that Robby was the last player on the bench." Treatment maintained that Kobe never looked away from Schwartz during the next 75 minutes of practice, and as he drove home that night, he couldn't get over what he'd seen, the intensity of Kobe's reaction to what anybody else would consider as a meaningless loss in just another scrimmage. He came to a halt at a traffic light and grasped the gravity of the situation. That is what sets him apart. That is what sets him apart from the crowd.

"I think some of the kids were a little intimidated," Treatman explained.

How could Kobe's teammates handle Roman Catholic if they couldn't handle his aggression? So, how about St. Anthony? What about the district and state playoffs, Chester? What if, on the other hand, the other players were overconfident because they trusted Kobe to bail them out? Downer saw risks everywhere, even one caused by the team's ostensibly improved performance. Downer was concerned about Kobe's reaction if the coaches couldn't keep Matkov on the team in good conscience because of the Aces' general surge in talent.

"What am I going to do with this guy?" Downer asked Egan a question. "He can't really play for us, but he's Kobe's best friend."

"Cut him," Egan said. "Kobe probably won't notice for at least two weeks."

As it turned out, Matkov departed the team before Downer could discharge him. Two weeks later, Kobe looked around practice and wondered, "What happened to Matkov?"

Over the preceding two years, Joe Bryant had frequently assured Speedy Morris, "If Kobe goes to college, he'll go to La Salle." Joe said it to placate his employer and keep his job, but nothing had been fixed, and nothing would be resolved, as far as Kobe and Joe were concerned. Morris and Joe's relationship had broken down, which Morris was completely ignorant of. Joe continued to talk with Jeremy Treatman once a week, whispering into his office phone so Morris wouldn't hear, and kept Treatman up to date on all of Sonny Vaccaro's conversations. Joe, who was juggling being a parent and a recruiter, didn't like the tone of Morris' questions about Kobe. "He was asking me as a recruiter," Joe explained once, "and I didn't appreciate that." On October 5, 1995, the Philadelphia Daily News released a story titled, "La Salle, NBA top Kobe Bryant's list," to which Kobe snickered in mockery. He'd told Pam, "Mom, there's no way in hell I'm going to La Salle, no way in hell," and Joe, "Dad, it's not on you."

The media... It was simple to conceal his genuine feelings from them; simply smile and deflect and emphasise how much he had learned from his father about the process, how much fun it was, and how he was taking it all in. The chances of him changing his mind were slim, but he was content to keep his options open—"Never say never, may go down there, have the best time of your life"—and listening to him answer questions about his decision revealed that he relished the speculation. To him, stringing people along and keeping them guessing was a game. He was a fan of Villanova, Michigan, and Arizona. Villanova? It would be great to play with Tim Thomas close to home. Michigan? He was a huge fan of Jalen Rose and the original Fab Five. Arizona? Stephen Jackson, one of their recruiters, had become a buddy of his. But none of those connections or reasons were strong or profound enough to persuade him to attend any of those schools, and with the exception of Duke and Krzyzewski, whom he spoke with on the phone here and there, even college basketball's blue bloods were standing on tiptoes outside Kobe's window, hoping to catch his eye. Kentucky? Rick Pitino couldn't persuade Kobe to come to Lexington, so he did what he believed was the next best thing: he flew Gregg Downer down for a weekend. Downer, who had long liked Pitino, went to watch the Wildcats practice and explore the university and town, but it didn't do much to persuade Kobe to change his mind. What about North Carolina? Dean Smith had sent Kobe a recruitment letter, and he had been so excited—Dean Smith!—that he had opened the mail in English class while his teacher was droning on. But if he went to North Carolina, he would be going to Michael Jordan's alma mater, and as much as he adored and admired Jordan, how could he, Kobe Bryant, have his own identity there? Besides, Smith had gotten right to the point: We know you're going pro, but if you change your mind, there's a scholarship waiting for you here.

Take Downer for example. Downer was not fooled when Kobe adhered to his advice without specifically stating that he would go pro right away. He could sense which way Kobe was going and what his objectives were, and he voiced his concerns to him: "I know you'll be a great player in the NBA eventually." But right now, you have the world in your hands, and if you go to the NBA and don't deliver, you'll lose it. You won't have to worry if you go to college. Kobe was unconcerned. He wanted people to be sceptical of him. "I didn't want to come in like Shaquille O'Neal, or maybe Chris Webber, who had all these expectations riding on them," he explained. "Even if they're performing admirably, it's never going to be enough because they'll never meet the expectations that people place on them." I just want to creep up on folks slowly. The next thing you'll hear is, 'Oh, wow, he's doing fantastic.' That's how I'd like to always be. I want to sneak up on somebody like a shark."

Kobe wasn't the only one who was sneaking up on individuals and holding secrets. Sonny Vaccaro's hints, clues, and advances to him and his family formed the foundation of a strategy so clever and covert that a British spy would have been envious. First, Vaccaro persuaded Adidas president Peter Moore of a theory: In order to sign a significant player to a major endorsement agreement, Vaccaro needed to be geographically closer to where most of them were, which was within a couple of hours of New York. So Adidas arranged for Vaccaro and his wife, Pam, to relocate and reside in Manhattan for nine months, allowing him and his associate Gary Charles to return to work. They'd go down to Philadelphia under the guise of going to Villanova to see Kerry Kittles play, and then meet Joe for lunch or a discussion at the Pavilion after the game. Joe, on the other hand, would drive up to New York or New Jersey to meet them. "If I had gone to the Bryants' house," Vaccaro explained, "there would have been something like 'Sonny Vaccaro is on the move' or something." I didn't want to give anything away." Vaccaro had never attended a Lower Merion game. He wasn't required to. Charles served as both his ears and eyes. "Around Christmastime," Vaccaro explained, "I knew it was going to be Kobe." Nobody else was aware. Nobody, including everyone in Philadelphia, expected him to go pro. I knew." Arn Tellem, his agent, was waiting for him. All of the plans could be formalised later. But who knew Kobe would make millions from his contract? Maybe there'd be something for Joe and the other folks in Kobe's sphere, like the Lower Merion Aces. Sure enough, Adidas delivered boxes of uniforms, warm-ups, and travel gear to the high school one day, all for the guys' basketball team.

Donnie Carr fidgeted in a classroom desk at Roman Catholic High School, unable to concentrate, rivulets of sweat slicking his palms, hours before the brightest night of his basketball life. All he could think about was his team's game against Lower Merion that night, against the buddy and competitor Carr had always held up as the benchmark by which to gauge his own abilities as a ballplayer. I'm sure Kobe will bring his A-game. I'm hoping to bring mine. All of these people will be present. I'm hoping I don't make a mistake. I'm hoping I don't mess up.

The Aces had won their first game, defeating Upper Darby by twelve points, with Kobe easing into the season with an eighteen-point performance. When compared to this game, the game versus a Central League foe might as well have been an exhibition. This one, at Drexel University's Physical Education Athletic Center, has an expectant hum to it, especially on the La Salle University campus. Joe Bryant had been recruiting Carr for the Explorers, and the prospect of the game's two stars, Kobe and Donnie, teaming up the following year was too exciting for those associated with La Salle to ignore, even if it was a pipe dream, unbeknownst to anyone unfamiliar with Kobe's intentions. There were fifteen teens and young men from Carr's area in South Philadelphia among the fifteen hundred spectators at the game—the Center held just over twenty-five hundred—all of whom were unconvinced that he could hold his own against Kobe. "They didn't realise Kobe and I would go at it all the time," he explained. "They'd heard all about Kobe and were coming to see me get destroyed."

Instead, they witnessed a duel that would go down in Philadelphia basketball history as a forever game—pro, college, high school, and pickup. Kobe scored thirteen points in the first half while guarding Carr one-on-one and facing a triangle-and-two defence set by Roman Catholic coach Dennis Sneddon to contain Kobe and Dan Pangrazio. Carr had nineteen, a string of dunks and jump-stop pull-ups, his friends in the stands now ragging and shouting at Kobe after each basket, Kobe yammering back, and as Carr sprinted off the court at halftime, roaring like a gladiator, Roman leading by three, he passed Joe Bryant, who was seated near a bleacher row of sportswriters and scouts.

"Yo, Donnie, just take it easy," Joe advised.

"Man," Donnie remarked, "if he's a pro, I'm a pro, too."

Carr maintained his vigour throughout the second half, finishing with 34 points, allowing Roman to retain a comfortable lead over the

Aces, and he received more help from his teammates than Kobe did from his. Griffin got 12 points and 12 rebounds, but he was the only Aces player to score in double figures other than Kobe. Pangrazio was shut down by Roman's triangle-and-two; he finished with only seven points. Kobe finished with thirty points, but it was a difficult thirty. He took 29 shots, missing five of his last six, then chased Carr around the court until he was exhausted. After the 67-61 Roman triumph, the pals hugged, and Kobe leaned in close to say something into Carr's ear.

"Great job, man," he exclaimed. "Congratulations. This game was well deserved by you. What do you think, man? Why don't we all go to La Salle and do it? Who could stop us two if we worked together?"

"Let's do it," Carr responded, although he wasn't convinced Kobe was sincere. Joe, he suspected, had inserted those remarks in Kobe's mouth as a recruiting tactic. When Ted Silary, the Philadelphia Daily News' longtime high school sports beat writer, probed Joe and Kobe on their future plans, both were cautious. Could Kobe and Carr end up together at La Salle? "That would be pretty nasty," Joe added, "if it ever happened." Kobe assured Silary that he would keep his plans hidden until the end of the season. "But if I happen to wake up one morning after having a dream and I know what I want to do for sure," he continued, "I'll go up to my dad and say, 'I'm ready to tell all.'"

As a result, the huge disclosure from Kobe was missing from the following morning's Daily News. Instead, it included an article by John Smallwood, the city's lone Black sports columnist. Smallwood contended, under the heading BRYANT ISN'T READY FOR THE NBA YET, that if Kobe were truly capable of playing professionally in a year, "he should be that much better than Carr, a solid Division I prospect.... If Kobe Bryant enters the NBA today, he will be a late first-round pick at most, and he may not be heard from again."

I made up my mind that if we were going to become a team that would win a state championship, I had to be the right kind of leader, and that meant respecting authority and working as hard as I could.

—*KOBE BRYANT*

CHAPTER 5

THE CANCER OF ME

The country's greatest high school basketball coach and its top high school basketball player made time for each other in the bleachers of St. Joseph's University, to chat about what one of them had yet to learn and how much he could still extract from himself. The respect Bob Hurley commanded—for his career at St. Anthony High School, as a former probation officer, as a Jersey City native whose pungent Jersey City accent lent authenticity to his accumulated experience and wisdom and his willingness to share both—was enough to draw and hold Kobe Bryant's attention like a tractor beam. This was no trivial matter. Hurley's squad had just thrashed Kobe's by fifteen points, yet in the minutes following that 62-47 setback, Kobe buried his frustration and sought out Hurley for advice.

Kobe had 28 points on ten-for-twenty-one shooting from the field, and with four minutes, nine seconds left, he scored his two thousandth point in a high school career littered with them. That he scored so many points on so few shots, the most of which were jumpers from fifteen feet and beyond, was especially impressive, given that the Friars were unconcerned about his teammates, and for good reason. They all scored no more than seven points. "We were able to cheat off of them and help against him," Hurley explained. "He was a genius." He received no assistance from the other players."

Lower Merion met Central Catholic High School from Springfield, Ohio, in its first game of the tournament, a squad with a substantial height advantage over the Aces thanks to six-foot-six power forward Jon Powell and seven-foot centre Jason Collier, himself a future NBA player. The audience oohed, ahhed, and murmured for seconds when Collier stopped Kobe's first shot of the game. Downer quickly called a timeout, and Kobe made a demand of his teammates in the huddle.

"Hand me the ball." I'm going to step on his neck."

His teammates compiled on the first offensive set following the timeout. Despite being six inches shorter than Collier, Kobe posted him up, spun toward the basket, and slammed a nasty dunk as Collier fouled him. Drew Downer sat on the bench, stunned by what he had witnessed. Not only has Kobe done what he claimed he would do. It was on the very next play that he had done it. Despite the fact that Kobe's superiority over his colleagues and competition was becoming clear to everyone, it was tough for his teammates to recognize how exceptional a player he was and could still be. Brendan Pettit, for example, developed a broader frame of reference for Kobe after going to play Division III basketball at Wesleyan University. "You grow up watching videos of 'Air' Jordan, and you forget that he is a person, too," Pettit remarked. "Having Kobe as a classmate and teammate shows that he is a real person." But it's also amusing. As I progressed through college and throughout my playing career, I realised how unique Kobe was. "No dunk, no play, no number of points can ever impress you again." Omar Hatcher's perspective to basketball was altered by the tournament and Kobe's performance in it. "We got to see Kobe's game accelerate against some of the top teams in the country," he remarked. "He demonstrated to me that a good player's game must travel." It cannot be affected by location or atmosphere.``

While Kobe's game travelled, the other Aces' did not. Again, he was guarding the opponent's leading scorer, this time the massive Collier, and he was the entire offence. The Aces trailed by five points in the third quarter. To compensate for their lack of size, Downer moved to a full-court press, which neutralised Central, who went the final six minutes without scoring. Lower Merion came back to win, 65-60. Kobe scored 43 points, made eighteen of his twenty-seven field-goal tries, including three of his five three-point attempts, and grabbed sixteen rebounds. Dave Rosenberg was gaining more playing time from Downer because of his toughness and grit: Dan Pangrazio had twelve points. When he collided with another player or dived on the floor for a loose ball, his left shoulder would periodically pop out of its socket, and he would just pop it back in so he could continue playing. Even with a 5-2 record and a spot in the Classic semifinals, the Aces were more of a spectacular solo act with a dissonant, often disinterested backup band. The next night would show how out of tune they were.

THE KOBE FAMILY arrived at Myrtle Beach in time for the Aces' semifinal game against Jenks (Oklahoma) High School. Wesley Gibson spotted Joe in the stands, close to Pam, sporting a La Salle baseball cap. Gibson grew up a few blocks from Joe in southwest Philadelphia, joined the National Guard and the Air Force, and shared his time between the city and South Carolina with his son, Jarid, who was thirteen, in sixth grade, and in the arena with him.

"Hey, Joe, I remember you from back in the day," said Wesley Gibson. "Are you down here looking for someone?"

"No," Joe responded, "I've come to see my son play."

Jarid had heard of Kobe Bryant, but Wesley Gibson had not. Jarid, who read SLAM and all the scouting magazines and reports on the country's top high school players, was well aware of Kobe's outstanding performance at the ABCD Camp. His and Wesley's common passion for basketball was possibly the strongest relationship between a father and son who desperately needed one another when Nathene Gibson, Wesley's wife and Jarid's mother, committed herself in 1988. Jarid had been following Kobe around the Beach Ball Classic like a puppy dog, and now he had another incentive, a hometown connection, to stick by his side for the rest of the event. Jarid obtained autographs from Kobe and "Mr. Joe," and he and Kobe talked about their favourite cheesesteak joints in Philly and on the Main Line—"I'm Jim's guy," Jarid said. "And he liked

Larry's," Jarid said, before settling up with Wesley to watch the game that would change everything for the Aces that season.

Jenks High School had almost 2400 pupils, more than double the size of Lower Merion, yet for the first eight minutes, it appeared the Trojans didn't belong in the same gym. The Aces led 18-6 at the end of the first quarter, and despite Kobe's four fouls and his teammates' lack of support, they maintained a seven-point lead heading into the fourth. And they were up by nine points when Kobe—in the kind of moment that defined his Lakers career, when he believed so deeply in his own magnificence that he crossed the line separating self-assurance from self-absorption—took on three Jenks defenders by himself, ploughed over one of them, and was called for an offensive foul. He'd played thirty minutes, scored thirty-one points, and grabbed fourteen rebounds before fouling out.

"And we," Treatman recounted, "just completely unravelled."

No one more than the player who, because of his abilities and role on the squad, best complimented Kobe. Kobe's core burned hotter than everyone else's, but no Aces player was more tightly coiled than Dan Pangrazio. His background as an exceptional young soccer goalkeeper; the balance he brought to the team with his outside-shooting talent; the burden he put on himself and his parents, Dorothy and Greg: Those elements often spurred him to thrive, but with the added stress of Kobe's absence, they pushed him over the edge. He was oh-for-six at the line after missing several foul shots down the stretch. "And Dan never missed," noted Dave Rosenberg, who missed two late free shots after taking Kobe's place in the lineup. Jenks' Mike Bay went to the foul line for two shots with 0.4 seconds left in regulation, with Lower Merion still ahead 61-59. He made the first but missed the second... until the Aces committed a lane violation, giving Bay another shot. He sank his do-over, sending the game to overtime, when the Aces were completely destroyed. Rosenberg started the extra period with an airball three-pointer. As Jenks continued to steamroll the Aces, outscoring them 17-2 in overtime and winning 78-63, Kobe mumbled two lines over and over, loud enough for Treatman, who was seated next to him, to hear.

"No independence. No goddamned independence…"

In the locker room, Egan held out hope that the team still had time to pull itself together and reach its potential. "Guys," he said to the players, "you're just not as good as you think you are. Every one of you has to pick it up." Gregg Downer, too angry and distraught to say much more, asked, "Anybody have anything to say?" Kobe did: You've got to go after people! You can't back down to no motherfuckers! It was exactly what the Aces had done. Without Kobe, they had backed down.

You play the role of Kobe Bryant. You're the most talented player in the country. But you must respect your teammates in this situation. You can't be so brash. You can't face every team on your own. These men are doing everything they can to fulfil their positions on this team. You have to make them feel at ease. Everyone must perform their parts for this to function.

He turned to face the other players while pointing to Kobe. You have no idea how much stress this guy is under. You have to appreciate how hard he works. We don't stand a chance if you don't match his intensity. If we return to hard effort, prioritise the team, and don't worry about the end result or who gets credit, the results will take care of themselves. Take a look around the room. We have the potential to be an excellent team. In case you didn't know, gentlemen, this year we're attempting to win the state championship. That is why we have arrived in South Carolina. That is why we have Bob Hurley and St. Anthony. That's why we're pretending to be Roman Catholics. But things must change quickly. Downer was done. Treatman stepped forward.

Somebody says I can't do something, and I want to go out and do it on purpose and do it in an unbelievable way.

—*KOBE BRYANT*

CHAPTER 6

RELAX, I GOT THIS

The contrast between Kobe Bryant in the back of the bus and Kobe Bryant in the front of the classroom was startling. The team drove to road games amid a purr of low voices, a tiny buzz of conversation and pregame strategizing, and the white noise of the vehicle's hissing brakes and the rumble of its diesel engine. Kobe contributed to the sombre atmosphere as much as any other player: headphones on, a blank canvas, the notion of passing over a waterway no longer causing him little spasms of dread. There was a game to be won, and nothing else should have anyone's attention. However, once they arrived at their opponent's gym and kicked their opponent's ass, the Aces could let loose on the way back to Wynnewood and be themselves. Closer to the driver, Jimmy Kieserman might be telling stories about being a guard in the Big East or attending a true fraternity party at Miami, but the team's two dominant personalities, Kobe and Jermaine Griffin, sat in the last row—"Kobe and Dan Pangrazio being the stars," Dave Rosenberg said, "Jermaine being the soul." The team's comics were Brendan Pettit and Robby Schwartz. Oral Williams was known as "Sarge." Dave Lasman exuded a cool, Hollywood air. Kareem Barksdale would celebrate each victory by performing backflips on the court. Rosenberg and Phil Mellet were the academic standouts and tireless bench players. After the Fugees released The Score in mid-February 1996, Williams would tote his boombox, with its compact-disc player, onto the bus, and the album, with its reggae-rap grooves and swaggering lyrics, immediately became the soundtrack for the entire team.

We used to be ranked tenth.

We are now committed to one.

It felt like they'd be on top forever and no one could bring them down. After Downer chewed them out in his Swamp Fox Motel suite, the Aces won their remaining fifteen regular-season games, emerging as one of Philadelphia basketball's top attractions. "You started to hear rumblings across the county," Jack McGlone, a sophomore guard for Ridley during the 1995-96 season, remembered. "You'd hear about other Central League clubs playing Kobe and filling the building. You'd read about him in newspapers and SLAM magazine." McGlone was taken aback before Ridley's first game against the Aces that season, at Lower Merion, when one of the Green Raiders' assistant coaches warned the squad, Remember, guys, when Kobe dunks and the crowd goes crazy, it's only two points. "He was basically mentally preparing us to be ready for when Kobe dunks, not if he dunks," McGlone explained. "It's not something you're used to worrying about coming from a high school kid." In his two games against Ridley, Kobe scored 29 points in a sixteen-point win and 27 points in a fifteen-point win, but the sheer experience of playing with or against him was more memorable for McGlone and his Ridley teammates—and, really, for every team that faced the Aces that season, and even for Kobe's teammates. As heated as these suburban and neighbourhood rivalries were, they couldn't compare to the buildup, thrill, and atmosphere that erupted whenever Kobe came to town: centre stage, big game, crowd standing on every possession and going crazy when a player made a simple layup, the sight of children and even some adults lining up for autographs as Kobe stepped out of the locker room, a feeling never forgotten. "If you've ever played sports," McGlone explained, "it's something you've always wanted to do, and I gotta do it twice." That's preferable to a piece of paper bearing his name.``

Because Kobe and the Aces were a young basketball kaiju, smashing everything in their path, the fulfilment of those aspirations would have to suffice for those players and teams. Fourteen of those fifteen straight wins were by more than 10 points, and seven were by at least twenty-eight. Kobe had 48 points with four minutes left in the fourth quarter of a 95-64 victory over Marple Newtown when Gregg Downer called a timeout. "Look," he instructed Kobe, "just get one more basket." Fifty points is a good round figure. Then, to be charitable, Downer would have him sit out the rest of the game... except Kobe proceeded to throw five beautiful passes to set up five baskets from his teammates, just because he could, causing Downer to call another timeout. "You have forty-eight points!" exclaimed the coach to his star. When the Aces got the ball again, Kobe made a layup and finally took a seat. "He could be so stubborn," Downer later remarked.

Yes, he could, and he was filled with reckless optimism about the Aces' chances once the district and state playoffs began. Downer couldn't afford to be so casual about any game or result. Around Valentine's Day, Episcopal Academy's headmaster, James Crawford, called him in for a meeting and told him that because coaching Kobe and Lower Merion was taking up so much of Downer's time and keeping him from fulfilling his obligations to Episcopal, he would be fired at the end of the school year. What are you on about? Downer replied. I told you I have to see this Kobe situation through. I told you that from the beginning. (Crawford later stated that he couldn't recollect the details of their chat.) Never mind Downer's reputation or future as a basketball coach if he does not win a district or state championship in 1996. He's been given four years of Kobe Bryant and he can't do it? That concept, however, was incomprehensible to Kobe. He'd tell Downer to "relax, Coach." I got it. And he'd tell his teammates the same thing. We're in our senior year of high school. We're in our early twenties. We have the entire world ahead of us. Simply have a nice time. Play some basketball. We make an excellent team. "I'm telling them, 'Emory, Omar, Butter, do you know how good we are?'" Smile! Have a good time! Don't be concerned. "I got this," he stated once. "I'd make fun of them. They'll be apprehensive before a game or something else. 'Don't worry, I've got this.' They were fantastic. They relaxed a little. As practice progressed, it became increasingly competitive. Everything began to relax. 'Man, we're going to win this thing.'" He also had an answer for anyone who fell into the complacency that defined the team's play before the trip to Myrtle Beach. Dabney had a hip ailment that flared up like a Zippo spark every time he ran, but Kobe showed no sympathy, telling him that it was his obligation to play through the agony, to go as hard as he could until he couldn't run any longer. Dabney followed suit. Relax. I got it.

The Kobe in the classroom wasn't as assured as the one on the floor or among his teammates. He had approached Jeanne Mastriano about taking Speaking Arts, a one-semester course in which students learned, wrote, and gave speeches and dramatic monologues, and then criticised each other. Mastriano described the course's goal as teaching students "to know your audience, know how to reach your audience, know what you want to achieve, and be flexible in your method." He enrolled in the course for more than just the sake of having the knowledge. He needed it right away. Camera crews from ESPN and PRISM, a Philadelphia-based cable network, followed him around the hallways for documentary-style broadcasts on America's most recognized high school basketball prospect's daily life. When Mastriano's class went to see Ntozake Shange's for colored girls who have considered suicide / when the rainbow is enuf, she and the students sat down only to notice, as the lights went down and the curtain went up, that everyone else in the audience was turning their heads away from the stage to catch a glimpse of Kobe. Mastriano became aware of the public's obsession with her prized student for the first time. "What really hammered it home for me was when we left," she explained later. "I was unable to get him on the bus. He'd been mobbed and swamped."

He was used to being the centre of attention. However, the standards for Speaking Arts put him in a more vulnerable position: standing in front of his peers in a hushed room, each of them scrutinising and evaluating him, all in a setting where he was not necessarily the most gifted or experienced performer. He strode to a spot near the chalkboard, buried his hands under his oversized white fleece and in the pockets of his sleek navy athletic pants, and spoke about himself for four and a half minutes, pausing every few seconds to search for the next set of just-right words, never lapsing into "ummm"s or "ahhh"s, his nervousness manifesting itself as he shifted his weight from one foot to the other and swayed back and forth, humming

"Hello, my name is Kobe Bryant. My age is seventeen. And I've been fortunate. Not merely to reside in different locations of the United States. But also Europe."

He felt isolated when he initially arrived at Lower Merion, he told the class, and he used basketball to pass the time. With the postseason coming and Lower Merion poised to win not just the District One championship but also the Pennsylvania Class AAAA state championship, Gregg Downer needed to ensure that his players were properly motivated. Downer never had to worry about Kobe taking things lightly or failing to see the importance of a game or scenario. However, several of the other kids... He wasn't certain. Since 1943, the school had not won a state championship.... He had an inspiration.

Villanova had agreed to let the Aces practice in the Pavilion, which would once again host the district championship game. Downer offered Jeremy Treatman an assignment the day before that workout: record himself announcing play-by-play for a simulated championship game between Lower Merion and a team from the western half of Pennsylvania. Downer wanted to offer the players a taste of what it would be like to compete in, and win, a state championship. "I don't think the kids realise what we're about to do here," he told Treatman.

Treatment followed orders that night. He took out a microcassette recorder, the same one he'd used to conduct interviews for The Inquirer when he was writing stories. He chose an opponent that would be familiar to the players: Williamsport, which had reached the state championship game the previous year. And he started. Hello and welcome to Hersheypark Arena.... The hypothetical game, which Treatman created entirely from his imagination, lasted an hour. Every Aces player participated in the game. To win, Kobe hit a last-second jumper. Downer gathered the guys at midcourt the next day, had them sit down, and had Treatman play the full film at Villanova. The majority of the players were laughing and cheering. Treatman gazed down at Kobe, who was motionless and captivated. "I think it had more of an effect on the other guys," Treatman later explained, "because they weren't dreaming it the way Kobe was dreaming it."

When the recording was finished, Downer let the guys' enthusiasm die down until there was complete silence in the Pavilion.

"Now," he replied, "let's get to the game."

Downer's motivational strategy did not end with the tape. He had the numbers 27 and 53 embroidered on the backs of the Aces' warm-up shirts. The significance of the numbers was obvious: Lower Merion had fallen by 27 points to Chester in the previous year's district championship game, and it had been 53 years since the team had won a state championship. "We just wanted to send everybody a message," Kobe explained, "and especially Chester, to say, 'Hey, we're here.'" Last year was the previous year. This year is a fresh start. So you'd best be ready and bring everything. If you don't, we'll whack you.' That was a message to you that we are not intimidated and will not be intimidated by you." The Clippers, the district's top seed, were only one challenge to Lower Merion's championship hopes. Coatesville came in as the No. 2 seed, having only one loss. The Aces were No. 3 at the time, and Treatman took advantage of a pre-practice shootaround to poke fun at Kobe over the blowout loss to Chester. The district and state tournaments in Pennsylvania were different events; a team qualified for the latter by reaching the quarterfinals of the former. Lower Merion could win the district championship, defeating Chester and/or Coatesville along the way, only to lose to one of them in the state bracket—a scenario that would surely vex Kobe, given his friendships and rivalries with Chester's John Linehan and Coatesville's Rip Hamilton. So Treatman wanted to know how Kobe felt about the thought of meeting such great opponents during the playoffs, possibly more than once.

"Linehan and those guys are pretty good," remarked Treatman.

"I ain't afraid of those n—s," Kobe declared.

Treatman was taken aback by the comment. Maybe he'd been naive all along, but he'd never heard Kobe say that word before. He wasn't sure how to answer.

"What about Coatesville?" he inquired.

"I ain't afraid of those n—s, either."

What was there to be afraid of? The Aces won their first two district playoff games by a combined 27 points, with Kobe scoring fifty points and hitting seven three-pointers in the second win over Academy Park, piquing the interest of New York Times sports columnist Ira Berkow, who travelled to suburban Philadelphia to see the phenom for himself. In the quarterfinals against Norristown, which had a lineup full of players with the length and quickness to harass him, Kobe saved his only bad game of his senior season for Berkow, missing nineteen of his twenty-four shots from the field and fouling out with one minute, ten seconds left in regulation. Kobe's bad performance angered him for days afterwards, particularly because he felt it gave Norristown's players the incorrect impression that they had stopped him, rather than Kobe stopping himself. "I didn't want them to think,'Yeah, we shut down Kobe Bryant," he explained. "When the state tournament began, I wanted them to win and keep winning so that we could play them again and I could go for fifty, sixty, or something like that and show them, 'You didn't do it.'" 'I completed it.'"

The game in Norristown was likely the ideal worst-case situation for the Aces: Kobe was dreadful, but they still won. Dan Pangrazio, his Myrtle Beach nightmare long forgotten, sank four three-pointers in the fourth quarter, and the Aces won, 60-55. If there was ever a game they could lose, it appeared to be this one, and they didn't. They'd face Coatesville four nights later, with Chester facing Plymouth Whitemarsh in the other semifinal, and before he'd washed or changed out of his gear, Kobe knew he'd be playing in the Palestra again, and he started crying. "The road seemed really cloudy at the beginning of the year," he added. "I really didn't know what to expect." After gathering himself and exiting the locker room, he gave Berkow a quick quote—"And we go on"—as Berkow strode alongside him, scribbling notes and later describing him as a "young man, even on a lacklustre shooting night, properly confident of his talent and full of the pleasures of life," watching as Kobe hugged Joe, slung his bag over his shoulder, and jogged back to Wynnewood. "He had so much confidence," Treatman later remarked. "I thought his confidence was out of control." I learned a lot from him because I don't live my life in that way. He was the most self-assured person I'd ever encountered in any sector, and I still believe so." Forget about the court. Forget about the classroom. If you wanted to see Kobe Bryant as a teenager at his most nervous, put him in a room with a lovely female. He could swing between pally fun and near courtliness with his female companions, recognizing that his celebrity and good looks made him a catch but refusing to use those qualities in the way that a classic high school jock could. As the senior prom neared, he sought Katrina Christmas for advice on potential dates, naming female classmates and soliciting Christmas' opinion on them. Do you believe she'll be okay? Do you believe I should approach her? Jocelyn Ebron, his phoney girlfriend, would have appeared like the obvious choice. Except for...

"Then I introduced him to Kristen Clement," Treatment continued.

Kristen Clement was the Kobe Bryant of Philadelphia-area girls' basketball: a guard/forward at Cardinal O'Hara High School in Delaware County, just eight miles from Lower Merion, who scored over 2,000 points in her career, led O'Hara to three Philadelphia Catholic League championships, and played for coach Pat Summit at the University of Tennessee. Her nickname was "Ace," and she had been romantically linked to Eric Lindros, the star player for the Philadelphia Flyers—a piece of local gossip that, while not quite elevating her to Kobe's level of stardom, did make her more prominent and identifiable than the usual high school athlete. Treatman had interviewed her for The Inquirer High School Sports Show, and he told Kobe about her: lovely girl at O'Hara, amazing player.

"Jeremy," Kobe announced one day, "we're going to watch Ace play." "When is her next game?"

"Actually," Treatman said, "February 11 is my birthday."

So Treatman spent his thirtieth birthday afternoon in the bleachers of O'Hara's gym, close to Kobe. "At the end of the game," Treatman recounted, "Kristen does a double take." 'Oh, hi.' I observed them swap numbers and assumed it was simply a friendly exchange. The next thing I knew, he was on the phone with Kristen Clement, no matter where we were. She came to all of our games after that. They were walking from the bus together." The couple's fledgling romance faced them with the difficulties that come with living in the public eye. After the Aces played an away game that Clement attended, Kobe approached Robby Schwartz as the two of them deboarded the team bus. Kobe was due to meet Clement at a restaurant in Ardmore that night, and she was bringing a buddy.

"Would you like to come?" Kobe inquired.

"Of course!" says the author. According to Schwartz.

After they got to the restaurant, Schwartz realised why Kobe had invited him to be his wingman for his double date. "I just remember looking around," Schwartz said, "and everyone was staring at our booth." I don't think I spoke more than ten words all night. It was clearly a 'Come with us so we're not alone' situation." He didn't blame Kobe for being lonely. How else could he maintain his sanity in his social life? "Basketball was ninety-nine percent of his life, but he was as normal as the best player in the country could be," Schwartz explained. "Everyone behaved differently around him. If you were introduced to someone, if you met me—'Hey, there's a man who plays Lower Merion basketball over there,' you'd come up to me and say hello, just like any other person. But no one ever acted normally. They'd just say foolish crap, and they'd forgotten how to behave around him. Just come say hello! He's just a regular guy!" A normal guy who, in the spring, would have a normal senior prom experience, one would imagine.

On February 27, two weeks and one day after Bill Lyon's letter defending Speedy Morris ran in The Inquirer, La Salle University held a news conference to announce that Morris's contract had been extended for two years, through 1999. "Without that article, I don't get that extension," Morris explained. "I'm certain of it." There was no mention of Kobe Bryant, who would be playing in the District One semifinals versus Coatesville that night at the Palestra.

I definitely one day want to sit down with him and talk with him, and hopefully he can give me some advice ... so I can break all his records.

—KOBE BRYANT, ON MICHAEL JORDAN, 1996

CHAPTER 7

THE TUNNEL

Here was his chance, perhaps Rip Hamilton's last chance, to prove himself better than Kobe Bryant, and how could he know, as a senior stepping onto the Palestra floor for another District One semifinal game, what lay ahead for him and the friend and adversary he had come to love, respect, and, in the healthiest sense, fear? The gym was trembling and quivering, and spectators spilled into the aisles. Gene Shue, then the Sixers' head coach and now their director of player personnel, was among them, seated near the floor for Lower Merion-Coatesville, so many people, nine thousand or more, in such close quarters that Kobe would claim after the game that every player on both sides "was in shock." Hamilton, presumably, was among those who required a few minutes to adjust to the type of environment that would become more familiar to him as his basketball career progressed. Just two weeks earlier, he had verbally committed to play at the University of Connecticut for Jim Calhoun, who was also in the Palestra stands for the game, to see how his recruit handled such a high-pressure situation, to see if Hamilton could step out of the shadow that Kobe would cast over him for the majority of their careers. Yes, Hamilton would outperform Kobe in some areas during his three seasons at UConn and fourteen years in the NBA. An NCAA national championship—Kobe never gave himself a chance at one, but Hamilton did by enrolling at UConn. In 1999, he would win one. An NBA title—OK, Kobe would win five, but none at the expense of Hamilton. And when they did meet in the 2004 NBA Finals, when Hamilton and the Detroit Pistons defeated the Lakers in five games, he was as good as or better than Kobe: he shot a higher percentage from the field, a higher percentage from three-point range, averaged more rebounds and assists, and finally got some satisfaction from his rivalry with him.

And he now had him. He'd got him. Lower Merion led by ten points after the third quarter, with the Aces scoring the majority of their points either by throwing alley-oop passes to Kobe or by handing him the ball, spreading out to the four corners of the half-court, and letting him go one-on-one against whichever Coatesville player or players were guarding him. "It was a personal-dual type of thing" with Hamilton, Kobe later explained. "A lot of people said he might compete with me and provide me work. When people say that, I just chuckle and smile and think to myself, 'Man, I can kill this guy.'" But the Red Raiders erased that deficit in the opening three minutes of the fourth quarter, and when Hamilton's teammate John Henderson made a basket, Coatesville led by six with less than three minutes remaining. The initial meeting... Hamilton couldn't beat Kobe after he hit that 25-foot three-pointer and the six-foot buzzer-beater. The second meeting... Kobe had fouled out, and Hamilton was still unable to defeat him. That was the end of it. It had to be this.

This was not the case. Emory Dabney hit a three-pointer, then stole and laid it in to trim the advantage to one. Kobe found wide space in the Coatesville defence—how could he, of all people and players, find open space?—and banged the ball in with 1:43 left to put the Aces back on top. In the closing minute, Jermaine Griffin scored four points. "There's nothing like the Palestra," Kobe said after the Aces won 70-65, scoring 29 points and allowing Hamilton only sixteen, and setting up a district-championship rematch with Chester. "This was an incredible once-in-a-lifetime opportunity." Nobody had to inform Hamilton. He recognized after his first game against Kobe that he had never played against someone at his position who had both outscored and beaten him in the same game. Kobe had done it once more, for the third time.

"How come I always seem to lose when I play you?" Hamilton questioned after the game.

Kobe burst out laughing. "I have no idea," he admitted. The Coatesville Red Raiders would have to wait eight years until the 2004 NBA Finals for Rip Hamilton to find some sense of equilibrium between himself and Kobe Bryant. Morris' contract had been extended by the administration for two years, until 1999. "Without that article, I don't get that extension," Morris explained. "I'm certain of it." There was no mention of Kobe Bryant, who would be playing in the District One semifinals versus Coatesville that night at the Palestra.

The opening game of the semifinal doubleheader was Lower Merion-Coatesvile. Chester easily defeated Plymouth Whitemarsh in the second round, 65-45.

"We're happy Kobe gets all the accolades he does," Chester coach Fred Pickett said. We're pleased that he's an all-American. But we're going to put a stop to him. Period."

"He's a great player," says Chester forward Greg Hollman, "but he still has to slip his shorts on one leg at a time, like the rest of us."

"We're going after him," Chester guard Brahin Pharr says. "We're going straight to him."

The aces had two school days and one practice between their win over Coatesville and their rematch with Chester, forty-eight more hours for the buzz and demands to mount around Kobe and the team. Tom McGovern's daily lunch duty, his hour of keeping an eye on student behaviour in the cafeteria, occurred to overlap with Kobe's lunch period, and it became customary for a different disturbance to grab his attention. The cafeteria was on the ground floor, and reporters, television cameramen, and photographers were lined up elbow-to-elbow outside its large, panelled windows, just twenty-five feet away on the school's baseball field. McGovern had stopped allowing journalists into the facility, but they knew Kobe needed to eat. So they'd stay there, shooting, clicking, and watching, as if they were seeing Kobe in his native habitat. "There was a jock table," McGovern mentioned. "He'd go there occasionally, but not always. He'd also sit with any students who knew him from class. He was stunningly poised for his age. He paid no heed to the cameras that were rolling."

Practice provided him with some relief. Long before falling in love with the trip and living in the moment were mantras of the Mamba Mentality, he appreciated the necessary routine of preparation as a high school player. Marcella Shorty, the program's athletic trainer, assisted him in balancing three bags of ice on his body as he sat in her office the night before the Chester game: one bag on each knee, one on his right hand. He wasn't hurt in any way; these were just precautions he'd always done to maintain his physique in top shape. He waited an hour into practice before snatching the ball, driving to the basket with a couple of clean dribbles, and rattling the gym walls with a slam, as if to reaffirm he was ready for Chester. "OHHHH!" exclaimed everyone in the room, including Gregg Downer and the coaches. Later, after a practice, he cleared his throat to talk to his comrades, his voice deepening into a rich baritone as he aged. His goal was to lead them into the tunnel with him, into the state known to psychologists as flow, a state of concentration so intense that everything else in their lives would seem unimportant and unnecessary, a diversion or distraction, and would fall away like dead leaves from a rose cane.

The John E. DuPont Pavilion, located on the east side of Villanova University, appeared to be the scene of a national political rally or a Bruce Springsteen concert on this late-winter Friday night, rather than a high school basketball game. Its surrounding parking lots were jam-packed. A quarter-mile stretch of pavement between the arena's entrance gate to Lancaster Avenue, campus' main artery, was sealed off with yellow crime-scene tape. Those who had already purchased their tickets to the Pennsylvania District One Class AAAA championship game and were awaiting entrance to the Pavilion had to wait in a line that matched any backup on the Schuylkill Expressway in its length. Those who hadn't planned beforehand could only hope to find a scalper or two and pay anything from \$30 to \$60 for a seat. Or even more. Lynne Freeland and her husband, Michael, arrived at the Pavilion with their tickets already in hand, and he dropped her there so she could keep their place in line while heading to park their car. As he walked back to join her, a man approached him and offered him \$100 for his ticket. He declined the offer.

Inside, the arena was a mash-up of bodies, colours, and noise: students and parents, basketball fans, scouts, and media, the Aces in maroon, the Clippers in white trimmed with orange and black, cheerleaders chanting, step team kicking and stomping, taunts, and, dare I say, threats traded in the bleachers. Chester fans yelled at Lower Merion spectators and players that they were "garbage," "afraid to come down to the 'hood," and "scared to play the street-ball boys"; a student reporter for The Merionite meticulously recorded each of the remarks. Of course, it's reasonable to assume that the Lower Merion contingent retaliated in kind, but the tense mood couldn't be reduced to a conflict between a Black city school and a white suburban school. It was a struggle about money and culture as much as it was about skin colour, and Kobe was at the heart of it, threatening to steal Chester's heritage, a piece of the town's own character.

"The parents were trying to fight us in the stands," Dayna Tolbert, Kobe's companion, recalled. "Many people outside of the Main Line were envious that a Black kid from the Main Line was succeeding." That is not how the plot is supposed to unfold. It's expected that a Black youngster from the inner city will make it to the NBA. 'Kobe doesn't deserve it since he was born to a basketball player.' That was the case everywhere. That is why we were so protective of him. There were many jealous people and jealous parents in our neighbourhood, but it did not manifest itself. But the moment we stepped out of it—woah, it was bad. It was awful."

That fight, that pressure... None of it would worry Kobe. Nobody had to be concerned about that. Even Kobe's best, and the Aces' best, were feared to be insufficient against the Clippers. Gregg Downer had witnessed it firsthand, having coached Chester kids at the Keystone Games in Harrisburg, and having sat down in a Central Pennsylvania Denny's at 3:30 a.m. with another coach, the two of them ready to dig into a couple of Grand Slam breakfasts when a group of Chester players walked into the restaurant. Hello, Coach. And they ate their eggs and pancakes exactly like Downer, so what could he say? He wasn't going to say something like, "Hey, guys, curfew was at eleven." No way, because he knew what would happen the next afternoon, and what did happen: on three hours of sleep, after a brunch of Cheetos and grape soda, those same Chester kids would run forever without tiring, would ball out for him, as if they'd just had the most restful eight hours of sleep of their lives. And it was only a summer league event, nothing in comparison to a district title. Chester was 25-1, and John Linehan was a senior headed to Providence College the following fall, and even if the Aces managed to get the ball across half-court against him, one or both of the Clippers' six-foot-eight post players, centre Tyree Watkins and forward Garrett McCormick, would be waiting for them near the rim.

Kobe started the game at point guard since it was the simplest and most efficient way for the Aces to break Chester's full-court press. But getting the ball back into his hands after he gave it up proved too difficult, and the Aces weren't scoring enough to offset the Clippers' size advantage. Watkins capped off a quick break by slamming the ball with both hands. As the second quarter came to a close, McCormick showed off his precise shooting touch by nailing a ten-footer. Chester led at the half, 29-22. At the halfway point of their 1995 game against the Clippers, the Aces trailed by the same seven-point margin. A year had passed. Had they truly made no progress against the district's kings?

"Even though we had Kobe, I really always thought we were the underdogs," Dave Rosenberg said. "I'm not sure if that's the right feeling to have, but I certainly felt that way against Chester for the most part." Lower Merion was not an unstoppable force. We'd never beaten Chester before. They left such an imprint."

Downer needed to deconstruct Chester in his players' eyes in order to demonstrate that the Clippers were not an unstoppable machine. He had to make this game, the most important of these kids' lives, feel like any other game, and there was one feature that was shared by nearly every Lower Merion game: Kobe scored effortlessly, whenever he had to or wanted to, in any fashion he chose. Downer made a tactical change, taking Kobe off the court and relying on the team's point guards, Dabney and backup Dave Lasman, to beat the Chester press. Dan Pangrazio would remain on the wing, but Kobe and Jermaine Griffin—two of the team's tallest and most mobile players—would patrol the baseline on offence and defence, allowing Downer to replace the foul-prone Brendan Pettit with the gritty and tenacious Rosenberg. With their new roster, the Aces should be able to match Chester's speed and pace, while Kobe and Griffin should be able to keep Watkins and McCormick away from the basket.

The modifications altered the game. Kobe swooped down for a steal, triggering a 14-1 run in which he and Griffin combined for 12 points. Pangrazio lofted an alley-oop pass to Kobe for a thunderous slam with three minutes, twenty-one seconds left in the third quarter, and Kobe ended the period by swishing a deep three-pointer for an eight-point lead. He converted 10 free throws in the game's last 2:40; following a foul call on Hollman, he waved and yelled, "Bye, bye." With thirty-four points, eleven rebounds, nine blocked shots, and six assists, Kobe had earned the right to rub it in. The Aces partied at centre court before lining up to get their gold medals placed around their necks after Pangrazio tossed the basketball toward the rafters as the clock expired on the 60-53 triumph. In comparison to the adults in the program, the Clippers players were modest in their reaction to the game's outcome—"We will keep our head high," Linehan said. Coach Fred Pickett, noticing the Aces' joy and believing that the aftermath of a close loss was not the moment to exhibit doubt in his squad, opted to amp up the bravado in preparation of the teams' rematch in the state tournament, which both expected. "We saw them," Pickett reported. "They did, indeed, celebrate. Tonight they celebrated their state championship." Chester's athletic director, Randy Legette, told Delaware County Daily Times sports reporter Jack McCaffery, "Hey, we'd rather win a state championship than a district championship." Put it in the newspaper."

McCaffery accomplished this. Kobe read it the next morning.

Donnie Carr thought that Kobe would attend college during his recruitment process. Duke, most likely, since Kobe adored Coach K. The remainder of the ACC had expressed interest in Carr, including Maryland, Florida State, and Clemson. Bobby Knight had offered him a scholarship at the University of Indiana. But it came down to two local schools: La Salle and St. Joseph's. One night, he contacted Kobe to talk.

"I'm really thinking about La Salle," Carr admitted.

"That would be a great spot for you," Kobe says, "because you can go there and showcase your skills."

Carr realised there was a slight distance to Kobe's response later, when Joe Bryant invited Carr and his elder brother, Darren, to La Salle for a meeting.

Listen, guy, my son isn't going to college, Joe said Carr. Kobe will have the opportunity to be the first guard to make the transition. He's expected to be a lottery choice, according to reports. Don, I still think in my heart that this is the ideal school for you. You'll be on the field for forty minutes per game. They're going to pass the ball to you. You have the opportunity to do some incredible things here.

Carr scored nineteen points to lead Roman Catholic to a 57-47 victory against Archbishop Carroll in the Philadelphia Catholic League championship game on March 8, 1996. He contacted Kobe again on March 11. He was going to La Salle, he said, and he would make his decision the next day. Carr didn't say much after that, as if he was waiting for Kobe to fill the anticipatory silence... Neither did Kobe. "We talked about other things," Kobe subsequently explained.

Donnie Carr accomplished some incredible feats at La Salle. As a freshman, he was sixth in the USA in scoring, averaging nearly twenty-four points per game. Then he made what he subsequently admitted was a mistake by returning for his second year instead of entering the NBA draft. He was a local kid playing at a local school for a local legend, Speedy Morris, so he pursued the traditional path to success, the path that Kobe had scarcely considered. "You as a player are a penny stock," Carr remarked. "They draft based on potential." It can only go down once it reaches a certain plateau." He stayed at La Salle for four years, finishing with over 2000 points, although a bout of meningitis in his senior year slowed him, and he never matched his rookie season output again. He was not selected by an NBA team in the 2000 draft. He travelled to France and Turkey to play, and his luck worsened: bone spur surgery, a torn right meniscus, a torn left meniscus, and a ruptured patella tendon. Donnie Carr, who had once considered himself on par with or better than Kobe Bryant... and was justified in doing so—had lost all realistic prospects of a professional basketball career by his twenty-fifth birthday.

He bounced from job to job as an environmental services supervisor, swelling to 300 pounds and slipping into depression till a buddy gave him a volunteer high school coaching post. He worked his way up and was hired by La Salle in 2017. He's still there, working as an assistant to another of Kobe's childhood pals, Ashley Howard. The passage of time has aided in his healing, acting as a salve for the wound on his spirit. The past and its unfulfilled potential, as well as the continual comparison with Kobe, no longer sting as deeply. "It took years for me to get over it," he admitted. "The weird thing is, when people would come up to me and say, 'Oh, yeah, Don, you and Kobe used to go at it,' they'd believe it benefited me, increased my morale, and it'd destroy me. It transported me back to that time. I was right there with him, and he went on to become the finest player in the world, while I fell just short of my ultimate goal."

It was the "ugliest alley-oop of the century," Kobe later remarked, with Dan Pangrazio near the top of the key and heaving the ball toward the general vicinity of the rim, Kobe starting in the right corner, dashing toward the lane, going up, up, up, seeing the ball and thinking at first that he would catch it with his left hand and lay it in the basket, then bringing his left hand down, closer to the rim, and closing his

"And then," he continued, "everyone went insane."

He was creating at least one of these moments in each game now, moments that, even if he hadn't done anything else noteworthy that night, justified his reputation and the murmurs that had followed him through the first three rounds of the state tournament. This one came in the second quarter of the Aces' first-round game against Cedar Cliff at Coatesville, of all places, and it got them within two points after they'd been down by nine, and it's tempting to say that Kobe was making it up as he went along, but no. He wasn't like that. He kept his improvisational abilities to those brief moments on the court when he could raise a play from fantastic to breathtaking, tossing in just enough razzmatazz to let everyone in the gym know that they had witnessed him make a play that a high schooler should be incapable of making. He brought the ball down court shortly after that dunk, sizing up the opponent in front of him. I'd like to dunk again, but I might as well make this man seem silly. Juke right, spin left, complete the 360-degree turn, face the hoop again, give 'em the finger roll with your left hand, and you've tied the game. The levity ended halfway through that 74-62 victory, because for Kobe, this was all serious business. On the sixty-mile bus route to Bethlehem's Liberty High School for the team's second-round game versus

Scranton, he analysed Scranton's players' approach. He'd done his research on the Knights. They were 15-10, a young team that had defeated defending state finalist Williamsport in the first round, a result so unexpected that Scranton's coaches hadn't bothered to scout Lower Merion because they didn't feel their club was capable of defeating Williamsport. Scranton's players, Kobe reasoned, would be ecstatic that they had won such a major game, perhaps a bit too ecstatic. "Coming in and facing a team like us," he later said, "that can be intimidating." When the bus came, the rest of the Aces were the first to enter the gym. They were followed by Kobe, who was guarded by two security officers. The previous year's state-playoff loss to Hazleton had occurred at Liberty, and every sensory experience—the sight of the school building, the musty stench of the gym—jolted his memory and reminded him of that night. He gave the Scranton players a sly grin.

"When I walked in," he explained, "this guy from their neighbourhood gave me a nice little article." It featured their star player fantasising about the day he could guard me and play against me. He described it as a 'dream come true.' I genuinely admire him. I know I won't be able to stop him.' Small things like that. 'Oh, my God,' I exclaimed. 'I've got you.' 'Like a shark, when he smells blood, he'll go after it,' I added. He's going to go after it.' I could see he was intimidated by the way he looked up to me. I simply pursued him." Kobe blocked one shot, altered two others, and stole the ball on Scranton's opening four possessions. He dunk five times and finished with 25 points and 12 rebounds. Lower Merion won 79-39 after scoring the game's first 22 points. The Knights were more deferential than intimidated, grateful just to be on the same court as Kobe. "Obviously," their coach, John Lyons, stated, "that is the greatest high school team and player I've ever seen." Following that, every Scranton player requested and received Kobe's autograph, which both flattered and perplexed him. Didn't we just blow you all out? he wondered. "It's natural for you to be upset." But they smiled, and I signed," he subsequently explained. "It was fun. "I had a good time."

One more win—71-54 over Stroudsburg, Kobe with 36 points—felt like a formality, with the true excitement coming later in the locker room, when Downer and the coaching staff learned that Chester had also won its quarterfinal game. The teams would meet again on a Wednesday night at the Palestra, with a spot in the state championship game on the line. Despite his teammates' ecstasy, Kobe stayed silent, first in a corner of the room, then on the bus trip home. The newspaper pieces following the first Chester game, the Clippers' statements, had drained his enthusiasm for the district championship, framing it as a meaningless triumph. What difference did that triumph make, and what did it signify if he lost this time? Getting the better of Chester. Getting the better of Chester. It must be done. It must be done. It was all he could think of as the bus travelled through the night.

The Aces' first practice before meeting Chester was on Monday, March 18, and despite having an urgent obligation that night—one that could have easily distracted anyone else his age—Kobe felt he was the only player totally focused in the workout. A state championship, he believed, could be planned, prepared for, and won if he and his teammates performed everything as it should be done, if no one deviated, if everyone focused on the now. They'd done it for most of the season, but not at this practice, not to his standards. "We were just going through the motions," he explained, "not concentrating, not running through screens hard." He and Downer were irritated by the lack of effort, so during one drill, he and Downer "I tried to pump the team up," Kobe recalled, taking the ball around midcourt and considering the quickest route to the rim for a vicious dunk while little Leo Stacy moved in position to protect him.

Kobe took a cautious, deliberate dribble forward, pulled back, and attempted a crossover past Stacy. Stacy rushed in to try to whack the ball out of Kobe's hands, but the top of his head collided with Kobe's nose, knocking him to the ground. Downer immediately cringed. He had long worried that Kobe might be injured during a workout. But for months, his guys had prided themselves on their hustling, showing off their floor burns like war wounds to one other. How could he advise them to relax now? Kobe was dazed, his eyes watering, and he thought to himself, Oh well. I landed on my nose. I'll get up and continue playing. He attempted to stand. His face was covered in blood. Shorty dashed to the court, clutching an ice pack wrapped in a towel. Kobe pressed the towel to his nose, which was visibly broken, with his right hand. The entire team looked at him in terror, wondering if he'd be able to play in forty-eight hours. He took a stride toward the trainer's room before coming to a halt.

"Ball," he explained.

Someone threw a gentle bounce pass to him. He caught the ball with his left hand five feet past the three-point line. He turned to face Treatman, who was standing nearby.

"Jeremy, I'll bet you five dollars that I can make this three-point shot with my left hand," Kobe jokes. "I'll bet you I can make this shot."

Treatman accepted the wager. Kobe lofted the ball toward the basket one-handed, off-handed.

Swish.

He continued on his way to the trainer's room.

"The rest of us are just standing there," Robby Schwartz recounted, "like, 'What the hell is even going on here?'"

Kobe informed Shorty that he needed to return to the practice court. Stacy's head smashed with him just as his jump shot was about to fall. It irritated him that he couldn't improve on his game, since Leo Stacy—"five foot nothing, weighs a hundred and nothing pounds," Kobe said—had broken his nose. But Shorty and the coaches were emphatic that he would not be let back on the court. He had somewhere else to be, after all.

It was a night for Kobe to catch up with old pals, Jerry Stackhouse and Vernon Maxwell, in the Spectrum's home locker room, a couple of hours before the Sixers' game versus the Chicago Bulls. John Lucas had invited Kobe to the game in order to preserve and improve their friendship as the NBA draft neared, which was still three months away. Lucas had now interrupted Stackhouse and Maxwell's chat with an offer that Kobe couldn't refuse.

Let's go talk to Michael.

Lucas escorted Kobe to the visiting locker room. Jordan was surrounded by a swarm of reporters. Kobe slid up against a nearby wall as close as he could.

"Kobe," Jordan inquired, "what's up?"

Kobe had a peek around. Is there another Kobe in the house? I can tell he's not talking to me.

Jordan reached out his hand. "Hey," he continued, "nice meeting you, young man." Kobe had no idea Jordan knew anything about him. Did he recall their brief encounter when Kobe was in eighth grade? Has Lucas said anything to him? Jordan had heard or read anything about him. Kobe extended his hand to shake Jordan's. His hand is so... powerful... Kobe was unfazed. This person in front of him, this person whom the entire world worshipped, was a human being like everyone else. Like Kobe, he's just a basketball player.

Unlike their prior meeting, Jordan spent some time talking to Kobe this time. He told him to enjoy the game. With all of the pressure and hype, it's easy to become sidetracked, and the game won't be fun. Don't allow it to happen to you. Stay true to yourself. Everything will be OK if you have fun on the court. Jordan's final bit of advice: "Man, if it were up to me, you'd go to North Carolina." Travel to Carolina. He stated it three or four times, unaware that Kobe had already made up his mind about the NBA, that he had already told Jeanne Mastriano, "The window's closing." I won't be able to play against Michael if I don't leave right now." Without anybody noticing, the sands of power and popularity in an institution, in a culture, might begin to change. The Bulls defeated the Sixers, 98-94, on their route to a 72-win season and the fourth of Jordan's six titles. "There was also an audience with Michael Jordan on Monday..." Kobe's introduction to him earned nothing more than a throwaway word in a Philadelphia Inquirer piece a few days later. It would have been foolish to forge a stronger bond between the two of them at the time, between the world's most famous and admired athlete and a seventeen-year-old ambition. But keep in mind that only two years separated Jordan's last NBA title from Kobe's first. The transition from one to the other was more direct than anyone could have predicted in 1996, and by 2020, Jordan felt compelled enough to reaffirm his place in the sport, to remind everyone of his significance, that he collaborated with the NBA on the ten-part ESPN documentary The Last Dance. "What you get from me is from him," said Kobe during the series. "I don't get five championships here without him." In the interview, there is a minor but telling detail: As soon as Kobe says those words, he moves his right hand as if he is pushing away either the interviewer or the question, as if he is saying, Slow down. Don't forget about it. Michael was the first to arrive. Not because Kobe had exceeded Jordan as a player, but because he had surpassed him as a storyteller. He had travelled the redemptive narrative arc, destroying his good name and nearly his marriage in that hotel room in Eagle, Colorado; destroying relationships with who knows how many coaches, players, and peers before reconstituting them; somehow scrubbing away much of that grime to emerge as someone perceived to have matured, to have found the elusive balance between peace and ambition; persuading people that the arrogance and atrocious choices were not his fault. It was a more impressive trick than anything Michael Jordan has ever performed.

I can remember getting in an argument with one of the teachers in school, a substitute teacher. This is when I was a junior. He's talking about all this trash. We had just lost to Chester, and he said, "Y'all never will win a state championship. Do you honestly think you can win a state championship?" I'm like, "Yes." He's like, "You can believe that all you want. You will never win a state championship. There are too many great players out there, too many great teams out there. You'll never, ever win." I looked at him: "Man, you're wrong. Watch."

—KOBE BRYANT

CHAPTER 8

THE FINAL GAME

For the three days before the state semifinals, Kobe could have spent his time basking in the gratifying news of perhaps his greatest individual honour to date: He had won the Naismith Award as the best high school basketball player in the nation. But his thoughts were a swirl of anxiety and excitement, of possible outcomes elating and intolerable. So he fed his mind with familiar nourishment. As if he were again in Italy, learning basketball at his father's feet, he watched and rewatched game tapes of Magic Johnson. All of the tapes had one thing in common. Each of them was one of the four Game Sevens that Johnson had played in his career. (Jordan would play just two in his.) This time, he wasn't focusing on Magic's no-look passes and slope-shouldered dribble as he led a fast break, his precognition of where all his teammates would be on the court and when they would be there. This time, Kobe focused on something else: How did he handle the pressure? Did he let the game come to him? Did he go out and take it? How did he lead his team to victory? Then Kobe focused on himself: What if his shots didn't fall? What if his teammates' shots didn't fall? How would they withstand the crowd noise in the Palestra? How would they react if and when

Chester took the lead? How would they handle the adversity? "I was very nervous," he said later. "At the same time, I was excited because I knew it was the chance of a lifetime. I knew that we could beat them. There wasn't any doubt that we could beat them. We just had to play our game."

Gregg Downer wasn't so certain. During a Tuesday practice, one day after Kobe's collision with Leo Stacy, one day before the Chester game, Kobe had worn a protective face mask, and Downer had stationed Lynne Freeland outside the gym doors, having her stand sentry to make sure no media or students or onlookers caught a glimpse of Kobe's resemblance to the Phantom of the Opera. He planned to wear the mask during the game, as well. Should he? Would it make him a target? Chester's coaches and players knew nothing about the injury. No one outside the team did, and revealing the broken nose would make Kobe vulnerable to a not-so-accidental elbow. He didn't like the mask anyway. It limited his peripheral vision. But he might put himself at greater risk of injury if he didn't wear it at all.

Kobe answered those questions minutes before tip-off. "Guys, let's go to war," he said. "I'm not wearing this thing." He ripped the mask off and threw it against a wall. Now Kobe had no mask. He also had no legs. He could feel it in the pregame layup line. They were gone, limp. He tried stretching them out. He tried relaxing, hoping that keeping them loose would restore their bounce and spring. Nope. His defiant hurling of his mask against the locker-room wall had been dramatic in the moment, but whatever emotional inspiration and adrenal boost he and the Aces received from it had faded like a sugar rush. He missed ten of his fourteen shots in the first half, the Clippers making him labour just to get open. Every jump shot he took was short. After the game, he would deliver, to The Philadelphia Inquirer, a quote so colourful and nostalgic that he had to be thinking of his father when he said it: "I was making too many moves. There was too much jelly on my jam." He was dog tired, and though Pangrazio sank two three-pointers and had nine points, John Linehan was too often preventing Lower Merion from running its offence. Linehan had five steals in the first quarter alone. Chester led by two at halftime. The lead felt larger.

Now Kobe had a choice to make and a conundrum to solve. If he continued to remain on the perimeter, he would reduce the risk that a stray elbow or forearm would strike him in his broken nose and knock him out of the game. But if he continued shooting as he had been, every jumper grazing or clanking off the front of the rim, the Aces would have no chance to come back. "At halftime, I just regrouped," he said later. "I worked too hard to get in shape in the off-season. I'm not losing this because I'm tired. I just pushed myself. I said, 'I may be tired, but I've got to attack the rim.'"

It took him until the third quarter to demonstrate his dominance, driving to the basket and dunking to give the Aces a 41-39 advantage. He had only made four of his 10 shots in the session, but an important piece of information had emerged: The officials were calling an especially close game—at least, against Chester—and the more frequently Kobe went to the basket, the more likely it was that he could pile up easy points at the foul line. Settling for jump shots was no longer an option for him, and his constant pursuit of the goal drew Chester's defensive focus and alignment toward him, creating opportunities for his teammates. Lower Merion led 61-56 after Emory Dabney sank a three-pointer with 1:19 remaining in regulation.

Then the meltdown started. Linehan converted a free throw. On the next inbounds play, Kobe delivered a soft pass to Pangrazio, who fouled Linehan in the process. Linehan converted both free throws. The lead was now down to two. Dabney grabbed the inbounds pass and, as if he couldn't get rid of the ball quick enough, tossed a pass into the maw of the Chester press for Pangrazio. Another heist. When a Clippers player missed a jump shot, Pangrazio took two steps backward, anticipating that the Aces would grab the rebound. The ball rolled out of bounds from Kobe's hands, and on his second step, Pangrazio planted his left foot atop a Chester player's sneaker.

His ankle twisted. He collapsed in a heap. "Is it broken?" shouted one spectator. It was not the case. However, it was seriously sprained.

Someone had elbowed Kobe in the nose during the scuffle under the basket, causing it to bleed anew. As he clenched his nose to stop the flow of blood, he looked back to see Pangrazio writhing in anguish and holding his leg. Oh, my God, thought Kobe. I misplaced my shooter. Four coaches ran out to help Pangrazio, leaving Treatman alone as Kobe and the three other Lower Merion players who had played in the game drifted back to the bench, zombie-like. Pangrazio was carried away on a stretcher by the training crew. Treatman had no motivational speech to give, and even if he had, it might not have mattered. Chester guard Tahir Lowrie sank a pull-up jumper with 27.5 seconds left on the next possession to tie the game. Panic was spreading throughout the Aces, especially among one player in particular. Dabney grabbed the inbounds pass around the left sideline and froze before sending the ball into the middle of the floor again. Garrett McCormick of Chester intercepted the pass and missed a short bank jumper, but the ball went out of bounds off Kobe. The Clippers would have possession of the ball and a chance to win. They ordered a timeout. Dabney was losing it, hot tears welling up in his eyes, the cheers and cries of the Palestra crowd coming down on him. Kobe could picture what he was thinking: God, the season is right around the corner, and I'm squandering the ball. But before Kobe or anybody else on the team could soothe Dabney, Drew Downer dashed over and yelled at the sophomore guard above the din.

"NOT RIGHT NOW! WE WILL NOT GO DOWN LIKE THIS. DON'T YOU EVER GIVE UP ON ME! DON'T STOP NOW. ONE MORE TRY! DO NOT STOP!"

Dabney might not have recovered if Kobe or any other coach had... supported... him in that way. But Drew was able to reach Dabney, motivate him, and relate to him in a manner that no one else on the squad could. Drew was the one who jolted Dabney out of his academic slump when he missed those three games early in the season. "He had to pull me aside and say, 'Emory, what the fuck are you doing?'" Some children struggle and have problems, but you do not. "You're just lying," Dabney recalled. "I had to tell myself, 'You know what? He's correct.'" After the timeout, Chester swung the ball twice near the top of the key, landing in the hands of Linehan on the right side of the floor, 45 feet from the hoop. Fred Pickett had called a set play in the Clippers' huddle that prompted Linehan to give up the ball. However, Kobe had returned to the lane's middle to protect the rim and give rebounding support, and Linehan noticed that the player guarding him one-on-one was Dabney. He made the decision not to run the play. He intended to win the game by himself because he knew he was up against a weak opponent. He dribbled to his right before crossing to his left. Dabney clung to Linehan's right hip like a cop's belt-clipped walkie-talkie. Linehan raised to shoot as he approached the foul line. Dabney, who was two inches taller than him, jumped beside him, reached up with his left hand, and deflected the shot. As the regulation clock expired, the ball bounded across the half-court line.

Kobe dashed back to the bench, his right fist up in the air. We're not going to lose this game. No way, no how. He split a double-team, burrowed into the lane, and dropped in a leaner with two minutes left in overtime to put Lower Merion ahead, 67-65. He hit two free throws to increase the margin to four points. Linehan missed a three-pointer with less than twenty seconds remaining, and Dabney retrieved the ball and handed it to Kobe, who tucked it under his right arm, a few feet near the baseline, the length of the court ahead of him. He may wait for a foul by a Chester player to stop the clock. If the Clippers were ready to give up, he might finish the game by passing to a teammate or dribbling around the backcourt himself. He didn't do either of them. All those earlier games, when Kobe went side to side, behind his back, and around, when he treated rival players like traffic cones, when Gregg Downer warned him about embarrassing his opponents just because he could: Those flashes and superfluous ostentation would suddenly disclose their purpose and utility. He got to half-court in three dribbles. Linehan attempted one last desperate steal. Kobe shoved his way past him. Two Chester post players stepped up to meet Kobe over the three-point line in an attempt to obstruct his approach to the basket. He shake-dribbled and darted between them, batting the ball in front of him, before they could secure position. To Gregg Downer, it was the quintessential Kobe performance, with everything on display: lateral movement, agility, and passion. The rim is there. I'll be there. You're not going to stop me. When Kobe soared, the baggy white T-shirt he wore under his tank top billowed like a skydiver's flying suit because he caught up to the ball just inside the foul line and didn't take another dribble. As Kobe blasted the ball home with his right hand, a Chester player shoved him from behind, prompting a tweet from a referee's whistle to mark a foul. His friends rushed at him, then dispersed, leaving him alone, pounding his fists, cupping his right palm and placing it to his ear to exhort the crowd, yelling only to scream. He raised his eyes to the scoreboard. This game has ended. He swished his free throw.

Kobe had scored twenty of his thirty-nine points in the Aces' 77-69 triumph in the fourth quarter and overtime. He had only made twelve of twenty-nine field goals, but he had made four of his final five and had missed only two of his seventeen foul shots. When the game concluded and he knew he and the Aces would be playing in the state championship game, "I had a big smile on my face," he said. "It was an incredible feeling." I could laugh in the faces of all the reporters who had written about Chester." In three days, on Saturday at 8:00 p.m., Kobe Bryant would play his final high school basketball game, which would be televised throughout the state on the Pennsylvania Cable Network.JIMMY KIESERMAN kept a basketball in his car in case he got a chance to acquire Kobe's autograph. After practice one day, Kobe begged for a ride home, and the coach urged him to get in.

"Would you mind signing this for my nephew?" Kieserman explained.

Sure, Kobe replied. "Do you want my high school or NBA number?"

He inscribed the ball with "KOBE BRYANT #27." He stated that his favourite number is 27. JOE BRYANT and Sonny Vaccaro maintained contact throughout March 1996, largely through Vaccaro's buddy Gary Charles. Adidas was on board. Adidas wanted Kobe, and Vaccaro and Charles could make that happen provided Adidas agreed to pay his father as part of the agreement. But Joe didn't mind looking into other possibilities or keeping the doors to them open. Being the head coach at La Salle was no longer an option. Speedy Morris was now well ensconced there, and when La Salle's season finished, Joe's connection with the coaching staff did as well. Sharia and Shaya began collecting their father's paychecks. So Joe spoke with other agents and other sponsors, and he told Kobe that if he wanted to go a different route, if he wanted to sign with Nike or Fila, they would look into it. Joe and Pam had created what they termed "Team Bryant": they, Sam Rines Sr. and Jr., and Ron Luber—friends they trusted to put Kobe and his best interests first. But Kobe had other plans. Fila had already signed Grant Hill and Jerry Stackhouse, and Kobe considered Vaccaro to be "the greatest guy.... He was present when Michael Jordan first joined Nike. He was present with him. He was there for his successes as well as his failures. He knows what I need to do to get back on track. Nike is the clear winner. I don't want to go with someone who is at the top. This is my chance to take Adidas to the top." Joe did the legwork. Joe gathered the contacts. Joe may give his son counsel and possibly even nudge him toward a decision, but only so far. At all times, Kobe was the one in charge. All that remained was to bargain and agree on a price.

In 1996, Pennsylvania's eight state championship basketball games— four categories based on enrollment, boys and girls—were contested in the same town, in the same structure, where the sport's best offensive performance had occurred. Hershey was recognized not only by the candy factory created by its namesake, Milton Hershey, and the enticing aroma that emanated from the factory's two sandy brown spires, but also by the fact that it made visitors crave chocolate. Wilt Chamberlain had scored 104 points for the Philadelphia Warriors in a victory over the New York Knicks at Hershey Sports Arena on March 2, 1962, little over 34 years before.

It was a record that Kobe would come closer to matching than any other NBA player before or since, torching the Toronto Raptors for 81 points in January 2006, and as he prepared to play in Hershey for the first and only time, he was confident that he could, and would, score 101 points if necessary. He stood in front of the student body at a school-wide pep rally and declared, "There's no way in hell we're losing this game." We're going to resurrect it. "I promise it." That week, he had what was possibly his best practice of his career. "I just lit the place up," he explained. "I didn't miss a single shot." I was ablaze. Nobody was tense. Nobody. Coach Downer, on the other hand, was most likely."

Yes. Yes, he was, as were his coaching staff members. Pangrazio had a boot on his left ankle. Omar Hatcher would replace him in the starting lineup, and while Hatcher would add quickness, a decent defensive presence, and the odd element of being left-handed, Pangrazio's absence and shooting skill promised to be especially crippling against the Aces' opponent. Erie Cathedral Prep finished 24-6, as near to a basketball dynasty as Western Pennsylvania—an area known for its love affair with high school football—could generate. The Ramblers had won the Class AAAA title in 1993, progressed to the state championship game in 1994, and reached the state quarterfinals in 1995. Marcel Arribi, their coach, had them execute a patient, structured offence that would lull opponents into a collective slumber before revealing a wide-open jump jumper or a backdoor layup. They'd have control of the ball, and within their man-to-man defensive system, they'd have a strategy for Kobe, whether to deny him the ball or badger him once he got it. According to Arribi's plan, Kobe would only have so much time with the ball and so many opportunities to score. The Aces' full-court pressure would be ineffective against Erie Cathedral Prep, and they would struggle to entice the Ramblers into a fast-paced, up-and-down game. To win, he and his colleagues would have to be sharp and precise in their play.

Downer's uneasiness was picked up on by Kobe throughout lunch, and he sought to calm him down. "Coach, don't worry about it," he assured her. "I got it. This game is going to be won by me. There's no way we've come this far, all the way to the championship game, to lose after everything you've done for us." But the precision that the Aces would need against Erie Cathedral did not apply to their late-afternoon journey west from Wynnewood to Hershey, a ride that was supposed to include a stop along the Pennsylvania Turnpike for a team dinner, a chance for the players to relax and relieve their mental and emotional pressure before the game. During the bus ride, Downer pulled for his motivational toolbox: He made the team watch the film Hoosiers, which is based on the mythical underdog story of Indiana's Hickory High School Huskers, who won the 1951 state basketball championship with a hard-driving coach, one star player, and a capable supporting cast. Kobe had never seen the movie Hoosiers. "It was similar to our story, really," he subsequently explained. An odd sequence of events destroyed the mask of comfortable assurance that Downer had tried to create as the bus took an off-ramp to the restaurant, just a few minutes away from Hersheypark Arena. Drew Downer awoke that morning with the flu or a variant of it. So, instead of joining the rest of the crew on the bus, he and Treatman drove individually, following the bus on the turnpike. Drew began moaning as he reclined in the passenger seat, dehydrated and light-headed. "What exactly do you want me to do?" Treatman explained. "Do you want me to make a pit stop at a hospital?" Drew collapsed without responding. When Treatman arrived at the restaurant, he raced in to inform Gregg that his brother was ill, at which point Gregg turned to the other customers and inquired, half-hysterically, "Is there a doctor here?" There wasn't one, although Hershey Medical Center was close to both the restaurant and the arena. Treatman stated that he would take Drew to the hospital and then try to catch up with the squad before or during the game. Kobe, who was sitting at the table with Jermaine Griffin, was oblivious to the commotion until he got back on the bus and asked why it was still idling in the parking lot. Drew is ill? What exactly do you mean, Drew is ill? How in the world did he get sick?

Nurses outfitted Drew with an IV to feed him fluids at the hospital, and once friends of the Downer family arrived to care for Drew, Treatman hopped back in his car and sped over to the arena. In honour of their flu-stricken coach, Kobe and the other players had inscribed "DD" on their sneakers, but they may have done better to add "GD" to their inscriptions. When the players were warming up on the court after Downer's pregame speech, Treatman noted that Gregg was not there. When he returned to the locker area, Downer was still there, sitting in one of the restroom stalls, his face wandered.

"Jeremy," he continued, "I'm afraid I can't come out." This game is not going to be won by us."

"I'll tell you one thing," Treatman said in response. "If you stay here, we're not going to win."

If he had, he would have been disappointed. He would have missed Griffin converting two turnovers by Erie Cathedral into baskets. Dabney also made a three-pointer before leading a fast break and feeding Kobe for a slam. Brendan Pettit snatched a loose ball and scored within. Lower Merion led by five points after the 11-0 run. After all those weeks and games of relying on Kobe to carry them, his teammates were shouldering their fair part of the load and more. After three quarters, the Aces lead 37-31. They'd be there in eight minutes. The way we remember things, the way we see and shape them in our mind's eye, is often the way we wish we had seen and shaped them in the moment. It's like retroactive foresight. I knew I'd marry her the moment I clasped her hand.... As soon as I saw the lotto numbers, I felt lucky....

"I knew," Kobe recalled of the state championship game, "that once we got up by four points, we weren't going to back down." That was the only thing she wrote."

Except that it wasn't. Lower Merion didn't score in the first four and a half minutes of the fourth quarter, and Erie Cathedral retook the lead, 41-39, with a brilliant set play that resulted in a basket. Dabney set up the Aces' offence after the Ramblers' game-winning basket. An Erie Prep player followed Kobe from corner to corner, and when he cut toward the foul line, a second player, point guard Julian Blanks, moved over to double him. Kobe intercepted Dabney's pass. Blanks snuck in. Foul. With 3:11 remaining, it's a one-and-one. Make both, and the game is tied. Make one, and the pressure will be maintained. Miss the first... and the dream will almost certainly vanish. Kobe inhaled deeply before firing his first shot. The audience would have thought it was over-the-top if a film director had orchestrated the basketball's flight and course for dramatic effect. The ball touched the front of the hoop, propelled lightly backward, bounced four more times on the rear of the rim, small jumps... and slipped through the hoop.

Kobe sighed once more and fired his second shot. 41-41, he wished. Hatcher, who had learned from Kobe at Myrtle Beach that a good player's game must travel and be excellent even in the most difficult of settings and environments, grabbed a defensive rebound, was fouled, and made both free throws with 2:43 remaining. The Aces were ahead by two points. Lower Merion led 45-43 with 1:22 left in the game when Keith Neis, the Ramblers' leading scorer with twelve points, back-rimmed a baseline jumper. After challenging the shot, Kobe grabbed the rebound among a tangle of bodies. Two Erie Prep players pursued and tormented him as he stood rooted beneath the hoop. There was nowhere he could go. He leaped and sent the ball to Dabney on the right sideline...... but Blanks rushed across Dabney's face, diverted the throw, catapulted himself into the row of reporters to keep the ball from getting out of bounds, and passed it to a teammate. The Ramblers had possession and the opportunity to tie the game. Because of a change in personnel. Kobe Bryant wrote this. So much for knowing that the game had been won a few minutes before. So much for everything she wrote. The Ramblers worked the ball around the perimeter, probing the defence in search of a decent shot, the right shot. Blanks broke through the three-point line and hit a one-handed runner from twelve feet with thirty seconds left on the clock. It smacked the rim hard and veered to the right. The lone Lower Merion player in the paint, surrounded by Blanks and three other Ramblers, tipped the ball to the corner, controlled it, and took off up court, dribbling with his left hand along the sideline, moving past Blanks, cutting to his right, away from another Ramblers player, until he reached midcourt.

What should I do now? Kobe had not handed up the ball, had not shared the glory, against Chester in a game where victory was already certain. It had been nearly eight months since he had bent ever so slightly to Sam Rines Jr.'s wishes in Las Vegas and given the ball up to a teammate at the end of a game, and it had been nearly three months since Gregg Downer had turned to him in that motel room and said, You have to respect your teammates and You can't take on every team by yourself, and so what would Kobe do now?

He never raised his head. He shot a pass forward, to the left of the lane, with no evident sign that he was aware Hatcher was ahead of him. Hatcher took one dribble and, thanks to his left-handedness, dribbled the ball off the backboard and through the hoop. "Kobe could have dribbled through that double-team," Hatcher said. "He put his trust in his friend to make a layup to win the championship." The same thing we struggled with early on was our final strength." Lower Merion was four points ahead. The clock continued to tick. Neis was called for travelling while pushing back up the court for a fast shot. He let go of the ball, which bounced once to Kobe, who held it under his arm as he leaped up and landed on both feet at once, as if stomping something. A timeout... a Kobe inbounds pass... a foul. He missed the first free throw but hit the second... an airballed Erie shot... the sound of a horn... LOWER MERION 48, ERIE CATHEDRAL PREP 43 on the scoreboard... The scoreboard showed Kobe with seventeen points, his season's second-lowest total, and Kobe, for once, didn't care... a dozen high school basketball players hugging each other in the centre of the court... Gregg Downer follows through on his vow to sprint around the court... Kobe embracing him... Treatman, Egan, Drew Downer, and Jimmy Kieserman are all enjoying... Pam Bryant and the rest of Kobe's family are in attendance... Kobe turned around, attempting to scale the security ropes and wires that encircle the court in order to reach his mother, sisters, grandparents, and...

"The next thing I knew, my dad was down there," he explained.

Mike Egan remembers the length of their embrace over twenty-five years later. It's what made Kobe's eventual feud with his family so sad for Egan, Downer, Treatman, and everyone else who knew them at the time. "Man," Joe told Kobe, "I'm so proud of you." And for 10 seconds, father and son were wrapped in each other's arms... two hundred... Egan thought it was a full minute, as if they wouldn't let go. WENDELL HOLLAND—late 1960s basketball great, judge, business executive, public servant, father, grandpa, the man who could credibly claim to have been Kobe's closest antecedent at Lower Merion—had watched the game on TV at his Bryn Mawr home. Holland didn't get the chance to tell Kobe how proud he was of his exploits until 2010, when he introduced him at the event dedicating the school's gymnasium after him.

"We got what I always wanted because of Kobe: a state championship," Holland recalls. "You have no idea how much that means to me." I'm such a Lower Merion snob. I'm pleased with what other civilizations and places have accomplished, but I'm especially proud of my school. Put all of those funny little anecdotes about Vernon Young and Chester together. Put them all together. I'm proud of that, and the basketball alumni are so diverse at alumni association and Hall of Fame events. Downer won games with this diverse group of players. Isn't that the way it should be?

"You have no idea how many people approach me now to discuss Lower Merion basketball." You have no clue how proud and sad this No. 33 was when Kobe died as a result of what he and Downer accomplished together. It killed me because he made my fantasy come true. He was the realisation of all of our dreams."

When the team returned to Wynnewood late that night, plans had already been made. Lynne Freeland had made a call to the fire department. Sunday would see a championship march through Ardmore, with students, teachers, and citizens lining the streets. And

Kobe and Jermaine Griffin would stand atop one of the fire engines, both holding on to a handlebar for balance, a dalmatian leashed up there with them. And when Kobe looked down at the crowd, he saw the substitute teacher who had told him he'd never win a state title. And he'd notice the teacher cheering from a nearby corner.

"This is all I've ever wanted," Kobe subsequently stated. "When I first arrived in high school, I knew I was a pretty good player, and I was determined to work hard to achieve all of my individual goals." 'Man, I hate losing,' I muttered after going four and twenty. 'There's no way I'm going through this again.' We improved the following year. We improved the following year. Throughout the entire process, I kept thinking to myself, 'I want to be known as the best— not only as the best player, but as the best player on the best team.' That meant a lot to me. I just wanted to show everyone that I was capable of leading us to a state title." That, however, would be on a Sunday afternoon. First, he and his teammates had a party to attend at the home of a cheerleader. A few players, including Robby Schwartz and Brendan Pettit, stayed all night before heading home at 7:00 a.m. Kobe Bryant stayed at the party for an hour before driving himself home, having scored 2,883 points in the previous four years—the most in southeastern Pennsylvania high school history— having accomplished everything he wanted out of his Lower Merion career, with the chance to enjoy one of his last normal nights of adolescence.

I've never wanted to offend anybody. I never was like that and never will be. I try to be as sincere as possible.

—KOBE BRYANT

CHAPTER 9

THE SPEED AT WHICH THINGS CHANGE

SATURDAY, MARCH 30, 1996

Tom Konchalski, America's most regarded grassroots basketball scout, was as devout a Roman Catholic as one could be without becoming a priest. Six foot six, lanky in frame, measured and kind in demeanour, he believed in the holiness of Sunday Mass and sports' power to form a boy's or girl's character, and he believed in both with equal fervour. God, he once observed, sent sports to young children to prepare them for their later years; the competition would stir different aspects of their hearts, and sometimes those stirrings would be unpleasant, but they would always be instructional. Konchalski's job in that mission, as he viewed it, was to find and assess young sportsmen deserving of that blessing. He had been writing for, and later taking over publishing of, a scouting newsletter, High School Basketball Illustrated, for nearly two decades, mailing out his findings to his subscribers. Hundreds of college coaches throughout the country valued those mimeographed pages for recruitment purposes, which is why Konchalski attended the McDonald's All-American Game, the nation's most prominent high school all-star game, every year. It was the reason he went to the 1996 game in the Civic Arena in Pittsburgh, as well as the annual pregame banquet the night before. And it was for this reason that he was seated at a table with Kobe Bryant and his family at the banquet.

Konchalski had been scouting Kobe since the Bryants' return from Italy, recalling that his first visit to a Boston Market restaurant—he had spent so much time on the road that he hadn't eaten at home in five years—had occurred on December 1, 1994, during a trip to suburban Philadelphia to see Kobe. "He had an iron will," recalled Konchalski, who died of cancer in February 2021 at the age of seventy-four. "He just worked extraordinarily hard." When you look at the Jordans and Kobes, it was their desire that propelled them to success." He didn't like the McDonald's game because there were too many players attempting to do too much and show off. (Kobe would be no exception, scoring thirteen points in nineteen minutes while playing poorly.) But the banquet was usually enjoyable. Every year, the famed UCLA coach, John Wooden, delivered his speech without notes, quoting Emerson, Thoreau, and Shakespeare, and all of the players wore tuxedos to the ceremony. "They'd all complain about that," Konchalski observed, "but who looks better in tuxedos than America's twenty-four best athletes?" And Kobe looked like a king. What a lovely young man he was." As the feast came to a close, with cake forks jangling against plates and coffee burbling as the waitstaff poured it into cups, the lights lowered and Michael Jordan's face appeared on a projection screen, offering a pre-taped video message to the players. Jordan told them it was an honour to be a McDonald's All-American. It gave me the motivation to keep working. Make certain that you receive your education. Then he said, "I hope all of you make it to the NBA." But if you do arrive, I'll be waiting for you. He also winked. Konchalski lingered after dinner, posing for photos with Kobe, Joe, Pam, Sharia, and Shaya. Kobe's parents and sisters had left before he turned to Konchalski, who had no idea Kobe was planning on leaving college at the moment.

"I can't wait to play against the greatest players in the world," Kobe said. "And I'll be ready."

He also winked.

SATURDAY, APRIL 6, 1996

Another city, another honour, and yet another feast. He was in Atlanta to accept the Naismith Award at the Georgia World Congress Center. Marcus Camby, the national college player of the year from the University of Massachusetts, was standing nearby. Over there was John Calipari, the national college coach of the year, also from UMass, who was two months away from signing a five-year, $15 million contract with the New Jersey Nets as head coach and executive vice president of basketball operations. When asked if he would follow in the footsteps of Kevin Garnett and go straight from high school to the NBA, Kobe shrugged. "I still haven't figured it out," he admitted. He could take a group of family members or friends out to dinner as a bonus of winning the Naismith, courtesy of the Atlanta Tipoff Club, which sponsored the award. When he returned home, he scheduled an appointment for him and his Lower Merion coaches and teammates at a steakhouse in Manayunk.

MONDAY, APRIL 8 TO WEDNESDAY, APRIL 24, 1996

As the date for Kobe's official announcement approached, and it became evident what his selection would be, Mike Krzyzewski called Gregg Downer to see if there was still time to persuade Kobe that coming to Duke was the best option.

"If you have a seventy-yard bomb," Downer said, "you've got to throw it right now."

Krzyzewski began a list of reasons why Kobe should select Duke. I'm going to make him the next Grant Hill... As a gemologist, I have a lot of expertise with sparkling diamonds... He gave an inspirational pep talk to Downer for five to ten minutes, and if Downer had been good enough to play for the Blue Devils when he was at Penncrest High School, if he had been a Bobby Hurley or Johnny Dawkins, he would have tossed his bags in his car and driven down to Durham in a heartbeat. But Downer wasn't the main objective of the conversation, and the target's decision had already been made up. Later, Kobe personally called Krzyzewski to inform him of his decision. Krzyzewski wished him success and informed him that he should call him if he ever needed advice. "I know you're going to be fine," he assured Kobe. "You have a great attitude toward the game, and you love to play." Krzyzewski would ultimately get the chance to coach Kobe at the 2008 Summer Olympics in Beijing and the 2012 Games in London, crediting him with establishing the work ethic and selflessness that would contribute to the United States men's basketball team's two gold medals. Calling Kobe "selfless" may appear to be an odd description. But, before the '08 Games, at USA Basketball's headquarters in Colorado Springs, Kobe knocked on Krzyzewski's office door and told him that he wanted to guard the opposing team's best player during every scrimmage and game, becoming so consumed with this self-imposed responsibility, with helping his country win gold, that Krzyzewski once joked that he was the only coach who ever had to remind Kobe to shoot.

Keith Morris was twenty-six, a new Prudential Securities financial adviser, and his father's strongest fan and confidant. So it didn't surprise him when his assistant answered the phone one day in late April and said Joe Bryant was on the line. Of fact, Keith and Speedy Morris hadn't seen Joe on the La Salle campus in weeks. Nobody had.

"Hello."

"Keith, I've got a problem," Joe admitted. "Kobe wants to go to the NBA."

"What's the problem with that?" Keith inquired.

"I don't know how I'm going to tell your father," Joe admitted.

"You be a man," Keith urged, "and tell him." Keith, on the other hand, didn't bother waiting to see if Joe would follow through. He hung up and immediately dialled his father's number.

"I was relieved to hear he wasn't going to Duke," Speedy Morris remarked years later. "For a while, I was heavy in prayer: 'Please God, I hope we get him.' And God always answers our requests. He occasionally says, 'No.'"

FRIDAY, APRIL 26, 1996

Oh, my God, how did I get here? Of course, Kobe had that question racing through his mind, gut, and who knows where else as he took in the spectacle surrounding him on a Friday night in 1996 at Madison Square Garden for the Essence Awards. Halle Berry, Tyra Banks, Naomi Campbell, Toni Braxton were all there, as expected, but how were Kobe and Sharia there, and how was this night going to lead to the answer to the most pressing and intriguing piece of news at Lower Merion: Who was Kobe's date to the prom? La Salle hosts a winter fashion display. That's how it started. Shaya was in the show, which was held in a ballroom of the student union building. When she told them he was her brother, one of them, Mike Harris, a marketing manager and promoter, remarked to her, "Well, tell him Boyz II Men want to meet him." Harris could arrange such a meeting since the R&B trio, all of whom were born in Philadelphia, was one of his clients. Weeks later, Kobe ran into Harris at a Villanova basketball game. The two exchanged phone numbers and became friends, with Kobe admitting that he had a thing on Brandy, whose UPN sitcom, Moesha, had just premiered. Harris quickly called Kobe and invited him to the Essence Awards, a gesture that Kobe, who was still lacking in guile when it came to matters other than basketball, might have felt was just charitable but had an ulterior motive for Harris. Here was an opportunity for him to break into basketball, to take on Kobe as a client. If only Kobe could build a name for himself on the national social scene...

After the award show—Sharia, who was as enthralled by the models, dancers, singers, and superstars as Kobe was—Kobe boarded a limousine with Harris and two members of Boyz II Men, Mike McCary and Wanya Morris, for a ride to the Four Seasons. Harris and Morris summoned Kobe to Morris' apartment. Harris burst out laughing as he and Kobe stepped in. What on earth is going on here? Kobe pondered. He then shifted his gaze to his left. Brandy was seated on the hotel room bed. Kobe's mouth dropped open. He laughed nervously as well. Oh, my goodness, you did not just do this to me. "How are you doing?" Brandy questioned, and Kobe could hardly answer, his brief "Hi" drowned out by Harris and the other group members' guffaws. He walked out of the room, barely remembering what he had said and confident only that he had disgraced himself.

Harris returned to his room and asked Kobe, "Do you want to take Brandy to your prom?" "Would you like to do that?" Kobe, of course, did. That was the simple part. Earlier, Harris had already dispelled a potential hindrance to his advertising campaign. Wanya Morris was twenty-two, and Brandy was seventeen, and they had been in a relationship for a year that was more than a friendship, but less than an open romance; Brandy and her handlers, too, were concerned about allowing her to reveal the secret publicly. According to Showboat, one of author Roland Lazenby's two biographies of Kobe, Harris persuaded Morris to go through with his strategy, allowing Kobe and Brandy to ride the wave of awww-aren't-they-cute publicity generated by one night together. That night, Harris contacted Brandy and said, "Brandy, Brandy, Brandy, my man Kobe wants to ask you to his prom." It would mean everything to him if you would accompany him." Brandy agreed. She merely needed to approve it with her mother, Sonja Norwood, who also served as her manager. Kobe now has a celebrity prom date, and he didn't even have to ask her.

Later that weekend, at the invitation of Boyz II Men, Kobe took part in a charity/celebrity basketball game at Community College of Philadelphia. Morris accompanied Kobe to the game, and after energising the crowd with a tomahawk dunk the first time he touched the ball, he made small chat with her at halftime, finding her sweet, the kind of girl he could hang out with and talk to like one of his female classmates. Pam Bryant and Sonja Norwood spoke later, clarifying details and ensuring everyone was on the same page regarding the prom, and Kobe and Brandy began talking on the phone on a daily basis.

"I admired her for what she was doing," Kobe later explained. "I knew I wanted to play in the NBA at the time, and I was going to be the young guy in front of the cameras and lights." She was in her early twenties. She began when she was fourteen, and she was in front of the cameras and lights. Aside from the fact that I enjoyed her music, she handled things really nicely, and I admired and respected that."

He wasn't spending time with Jocelyn Ebron anymore. He informed Treatment that he was still friends with Kristen Clement, despite the fact that they hadn't communicated in a long time. When his date's name was revealed, his friends reacted with amusement. When Treatment initially heard that Kobe was going with Brandy, he assumed it was one of Clement's Cardinal O'Hara colleagues, Brandi Batch. Susan Freeland asked him who he was taking to the prom during a study hall one day at school.

"Brandy," Kobe exclaimed.

"Brandy, who?"

"Brandy, Suze."

"Where did you first meet her?"

"One of the guys from Boyz II Men."

"Shut up!"

It was too much for Freeland to bear. Suze and Brandy. Boyz II Men. He'd stated it as if it were the most natural thing in the world.

MONDAY, APRIL 29, 1996

It was not Kobe's idea to hold a news conference to announce that he was declaring himself eligible for the NBA draft. Joe approached him and asked if he wanted one.

"Come on," Kobe exclaimed. "It doesn't really matter to me."

But he could tell it was important to Joe and Pam. While a formal announcement would provide legitimacy and weight to Kobe's choice, his parents were preoccupied with what he may say and how he might say it. What, after all, would such an event be if not a look into – or, for some, an instant referendum on – how they had raised their prodigy of a son? Joe and Pam harassed Kobe for a week after he originally made his suggestion, making sure he handled himself with the correct proportions of maturity, poise, and comedy. "I was kind of teasing them: 'Hey, you're more nervous than I am,'" he later explained. "It wasn't really that big of a deal to me." He didn't care where or when the news conference was conducted; he left it up to Joe, who chose a Monday afternoon. Treatman handled most of the planning, collaborating with Tom McGovern to prepare the gym for the expected gathering of reporters and students, as well as to notify media outlets about the event. Even when they inquired, he didn't tell them what Kobe had decided. Did he really have to? Would Kobe conduct a news conference if he was headed to Duke or La Salle at this point? Classmates contacted him throughout the morning, pleading for information. I have a lacrosse game this afternoon,

Kobe. Why don't you tell me right now? Kobe was as evasive about the NBA as he was about the prom, telling them he didn't know yet and would make a decision on the spur of the moment. The other students in his metal-jewellery class clustered around him, temporarily forgetting about the bracelets they were supposed to be making, while his teacher tried to listen in on Kobe's talks and ambiguous answers. "What are you going to do?" inquired his friend Deirdre Bobb.

"I don't know," Kobe responded. "What do you think?"

"Honestly, Kobe," Bobb advised, "you should go to school. Your gift will never be taken away from you. What you have is a God-given talent, and no matter where you go, you will be the best player in the squad. The NBA will always exist."

Lynne Freeland found him in another class and called him out. Gregg Downer would be present for the press conference, and he already knew what the news would be without Kobe having to say it. However, Freeland inquired, "Does Kobe want to call Drew Downer and tell him personally?" "Lead the way," said Kobe. Freeland escorted him to the guidance office, gave him Drew's phone number, and informed the counsellors and secretaries that Kobe required privacy. She heard him say as she closed the door behind her, "I'm going to play with the big boys.""What I wanted him to know," Drew added later, "and I would say this to him every time I saw him for years afterward, when he was an adult, was 'We care about you.'" We care about you as a person,' especially after he became the NBA's villain. I stopped attending Sixers games in South Philly because I was frightened of getting into a fight. I don't want to dramatise my actions. I attempted to protect him. I tried to act like an adult. Some strange-looking guy would appear and say, 'Sign this stack of magazines.' 'Who are you?' I'd ask. I had enough faith in him that I never asked him for anything. I didn't anticipate anything from him."

He drove home to get ready, skipping English class, with one period left in the school day. Pam assisted him in selecting his clothing. Kobe wore a white shirt, a brown silk tie, and a beige silk suit given to him as a gift by Ron Luber and his family, according to Luber, "to wish him luck in his next career." (When Luber bought the costume, which cost more than $500, the salesperson told him, "Did you know that his wingspan measured seven foot two?") To complete the look, Kobe wore a pair of black oval designer sunglasses on his brow. "That was my idea," he subsequently explained. "I've always had a thing for glasses." "I reasoned, 'Why not start something new?'"

The Bryants returned to school, arriving shortly after the final bell of the day, at 2:25, and parking in the back. The television camera lights burned in Kobe's eyes the moment he walked into the gym on a warm and muggy spring day, 74 degrees outdoors, turned warmer and muggier inside by the crush. Joe cleaned his brow with one hand while clutching a bulky cell phone in the other. Kobe inquired of Matt Matkov about the English class he had skipped. When his grandma saw the fuss surrounding him, she exclaimed, "Well, I've got to make my baby an apple pie now," and Kobe's ears perked up. "Oh, yeah, Grandma," he said. "You've got to make me a couple of those." When he stepped into the building, he had no idea what to anticipate, and suddenly the gym was packed, everyone came to hear what he would say, to hear what Kobe Bryant thought was best for Kobe Bryant, everyone there for him... and it was... entertaining. It was a lot of fun.

Rewatching the moment of revelation is a miracle. Kobe was absolutely self-assured as he stood at a lectern, a bundle of microphones at his chest, with the gym's rich brown bleachers providing a neutral background to frame him in any camera shot. His family, coaches, teammates, and classmates were seated and standing amid the journalists, with a large audience awaiting his words.

"I'm Kobe Bryant..."

Pause. He wiggled his head, as if he were shaking a defender.

"... I've decided to take my talent... to uhhh..."

Another brief pause. This time, he pretended to be indecisive, forgetful, or both. He lifted his left hand to his chin as if he was thinking about something, playing to the cameras, playing to the situation.

Then he broke out in a huge smile.

"No, I've decided to forego college and pursue my talent in the NBA."

It just took 19 seconds. A roar erupted. For a sizable segment of the population in 1996, a high school athlete holding a press conference to announce his future was regarded not as an appropriate, newsworthy event, nor as an indication of how much interest there was in such an announcement, but as a display of such blatant arrogance that it could barely be tolerated. Deirdre Bobb had arrived at the gym after finishing her classes for the day. When she heard Kobe declare he was not going to college, her heart broke a little. Okay, Kobe, she reasoned. You're smelling your own odour. But if that's what you want, I'll support you and pray for you. Neil Cooper, the rabbi of a township synagogue, delivered a sermon in which he chastised Kobe, stating that his choice would send the incorrect message to young people, undermining the value and usefulness of higher education. "All of this is warm and wonderful," wrote Bill Lyon in The Philadelphia Inquirer. But he's also seventeen, and the father in me has only one reservation: "I hope he hasn't ransomed away his youth." Kobe became an instant hot topic on sports talk radio, a microwaveable meal of fury delivered sizzling hot throughout morning and afternoon drive time.

"A lot of people probably thought that press conference was ridiculous," remarked Gregg Downer. "There were people who didn't know much about sports and didn't fully understand it." There were folks in that building who had no idea what was going on. I was aware of what was going on. This isn't just another athletic tall basketball player. "This is something new."

TUESDAY, MAY 21, 1996

At 10:00 A.M. Kobe was everywhere in a showroom in Manhattan's SoHo area. Kobe was dunking in four different spots on one wall, all four dunks recorded in six-foot-high images, all four photos with the impact of massive exclamation points. A highlight video played and repeated Kobe dunking, dunking, dunking, with a jump shot or two thrown in for good measure. Adidas had launched a new logo, consisting of three stripes that increase in length from left to right, representing advancement, improvement, and the future. One reporter went around the room and counted the logos: fifty-six. Walls with logos. Basketballs with logos. Chairs and microphones with logos. And those were only the ones he kept track of. More branding appeared on press credentials, personnel' clothes, and even the smallest flat surfaces. There was no reason for the corporation to be subtle. This was a coronation for the company's newest client. This was Kobe Bryant's king-making season.

"He's one of a new generation of athletes who will help transform sports in the next decade or two," Adidas America president Steve Wynne said.

The day after his I'm-going-to-the-NBA news conference, Kobe and his teammates flew to Harrisburg to meet with Pennsylvania governor Tom Ridge, and they did so in the same way that most high school state basketball winners do: in a car. On a wet day, they rode in a leaking school bus. It was the kind of thing Kobe was used to, the kind of thing that had previously grounded him and that he wouldn't have to go through again. He had been a player at Lower

126

Merion. Now he was a player, a representative for a sneaker brand, a rocket ship blasting through the ozone, and it was mind-boggling to consider how close this agreement, and the lengthy courting with Sonny Vaccaro, had come to falling apart.

Ron Luber had obtained legal opinions from a New York firm that had a branding operation and could, in principle, handle Kobe's shoe contract at Joe and Pam's request. Luber noted that the Bryants had a choice: they either stay with Vaccaro and Adidas, or they could go out on their own. The decision was nearly self-evident. Team Bryant members advocated choosing Kobe's agent at a meeting in Atlantic City. Vaccaro responded by laying out his ultimatums: the sneaker deal would be with Adidas, Arn Tellem would be Kobe's NBA agent, and the William Morris Agency would represent Kobe in any and all sponsorships and interests unrelated to basketball—acting, music, whatever struck Kobe's fancy. Then Vaccaro stood up and walked away. "Why would he want to stay?" said Sam Rines Jr. "There was nothing anyone could say, because he was in charge." With Vaccaro recognizing that he had leverage and the Bryants unwilling to let their best and longest-standing endorsement offer slip away, both parties agreed to a second meeting at Il Vagabondo, an Italian restaurant on Manhattan's Upper East Side. It resulted in Joe and Pam agreeing to hire Tellem in what Rick Bradley, Kobe's William Morris attorney, referred to as "a major contract by Adidas." Kobe and the corporation agreed to a multiyear contract worth $10 million, with the first year guaranteed at $1 million. (At one time, Kobe inquired of Vaccaro, "If I had gone to Duke, would I have been able to sign my own shoe contract?" When Vaccaro told him that NCAA rules would have prevented him from doing so, Kobe responded, "Well, I certainly made the right decision, didn't I?") A nationwide television campaign for his new shoe line—the slogan: "Feet You Wear"—would begin in August and feature him exclusively later that fall. In a relationship of such magnitude, Joe could receive his own signing bonus simply for bringing Kobe. It was nothing for Adidas to throw in another $150,000 for Joe in such a large collaboration. That it did. As usual, Joe and Pam, Sharia and Shaya were in the showroom's front row, cheering on their son and brother. Joe was there, telling reporters that the Bryants would follow Kobe wherever he went, as if he were a magnificent hot-air balloon and the family would cram into the basket underneath him. When challenged about the dangers of playing professional basketball as a teenager, Kobe replied, "This is the ultimate challenge." You will have the opportunity to learn from the finest. They're killing you, beating you up, and teaching you all at the same time. Only good can come from it." All that remained was to see which NBA team would select him in a month's time.

"We'd prefer the Lakers or the Knicks, Philadelphia, Chicago, or another major-market centre," Bradley added. "But obviously, we have no control over that."

Obviously. Right.

SATURDAY, MAY 25, 1996

The prom could be postponed. There was basketball on television. It isn't simply basketball. Basketball for the Chicago Bulls. It's not just the Chicago Bulls. Basketball player Michael Jordan. Kobe and Jermaine Griffin sat about all afternoon, watching Jordan struggle through a poor shooting effort (five of fourteen from the field, seventeen points), while the Bulls cruised past the Orlando Magic, 86-67, to win a first-round playoff series in a three-game sweep. The game started at 2:30 p.m. eastern time, and Kobe and Griffin didn't start getting dressed until it was over. Was the prom going to happen without Kobe and Brandy?

The game provided Kobe with some downtime during an otherwise hectic weekend. Team Bryant, particularly Sam Rines Sr., had taken care of everything, arranging for Kobe and Brandy to attend a Barry White performance and a fireworks display in Atlantic City on Friday night, then preparing another late-night journey down there on Saturday (with Brandy's mother along to oversee). The prom was being hosted at the Bellevue Hotel in Center City, one of Kobe's favourite and most recognized pickup-basketball sites. On Broad Street, outside the hotel's entrance, a phalanx of Philadelphia police officers and fifteen television news cameras awaited the arrival of the celebrity "couple," and they would be waiting for quite some time. Kobe dropped Griffin off at his date's house—Tarvia Lucas, John's daughter—before driving into town to meet Brandy at the Marriott where she was staying, he in a black tuxedo and a banded-collar shirt, she in champagne Moschino, her hair to her shoulders in flowing braids. "Man, she glowed," Kobe later remarked. They returned to pick up Griffin, Lucas, and Matt Matkov—complicated by the fact that Matkov's date had backed out at the last minute, so he would be Kobe's plus-one as usual—before a white limousine shuttled the five of them to the Bellevue, Brandy's entourage of bodyguards and stylists following. The TV reporters at the Bellevue stopped other seniors to obtain their opinions to the hoopla at their formal as they combed the streets for Kobe and Brandy's automobile. "It's not Kobe's prom; it's Lower Merion's prom," a female student commented. "We're not the class of Kobe," said another. "We are the graduating class of 1996." Such resentment, according to Susan Freeland, was misdirected. Of course, the prom wasn't just about Kobe, but "that magic and momentum we had as a class was because of him," she added, and none of the security guards, cops, and media were there for anybody else.

"He took Brandy to the prom for his image," Matkov once explained, "because he needed to go with someone who approached his status." Finally, it seemed as if there was a girl who disliked him solely because he was Kobe Bryant. That wasn't her motivation, because she was as big as his. She felt the same way. He was the type of person who didn't like her just because she was Brandy. He didn't require her. So they had something in common. That doesn't imply they were meant to be together.... He knew he couldn't go to the prom with just another stupid high school girl."

The white limo finally arrived outside Bellevue three hours after the prom had begun. Camera crews raced in. Cops and security surrounded Kobe and Brandy with a halo of space. Someone inquired whether she wanted to sing at the prom.

"I'm just here to have a good time," she explained.

The reaction of the prom's other attendees enraged Kobe as the two seventeen-year-olds ascended a marble staircase to the hotel's second story. "You had all your classmates bad-mouthing the whole thing," he subsequently claimed. "When we walk in, they're like, 'Oh, can we have a picture with you?'" Can we speak with you?' 'Get up out of my face, guy.' They were giggling. I guess I'm jealous. I didn't give a damn about them. They're not my friends in the first place. My friends are the basketball team members that are and have been close to me. That's what they are: fake pals." Sonja Norwood shared Kobe's disdain. "Everyone is asking her for autographs and pictures," she said. "She appears to be working." The irony of the evening was seemingly lost on them: they were whining about the attention that two young stars received at the prom... despite the fact that the entire ersatz courting had been set up to generate attention for two young stars.

Besides, Norwood was incorrect. Not everyone was taken in. Audrey Price, Kobe's buddy, requested a photo with the newlyweds but not an autograph. "It wasn't because he was a superstar," Price said. "It was simply more; I took pictures with all of my friends." It was only a flashback. It was done to cement that recollection. When I told Brandy that her clothing was lovely, she told me she was nervous. It didn't detract from the occasion in any way. Everyone went about their business as usual. It was still just like any other prom."

Brandy headed back to Los Angeles after her second night in Atlantic City with Kobe. According to one Philadelphia TV station, the prom was her first date. Wanya Morris would have been shocked to learn such a storybook detail.

JUNE 1996

Kobe Bryant spent his last day as an official Lower Merion student and his first night as an official Lower Merion alumnus at Lower Merion. Following their commencement ceremony, the seniors gathered within the school building's walls, where they would be locked inside for an all-night party—dancing, swimming, obstacle courses, socialising—a measure taken to encourage them to remain together and avoid underage drinking, drunken driving, or any other reckless behaviour. One senior toted a video camera around, conducting faux interviews with the graduates, and when the camera turned to Kobe, he came up with a four-line rap song, apparently off the top of his head.

My beeper is beeping

So let me quick pause

As I grab the microphone

For all y'all

Half the gymnasium had been partitioned off into a dance club with a DJ. There, Kobe lowered himself to the floor, curled himself up like a turtle, and spun himself on his back, breakdancing to Kool & the Gang's "Jungle Boogie." He took off his T-shirt, his torso resembling old-fashioned bottles of Coca-Cola stacked on their sides, and, still holding the microphone, grooved and lip-synced to LL Cool J's "Doin' It."

No doubt, I'm the playa that you're talkin' about ...

Right, I'm in the zone

One of a kind when it's time to do mine

In another section of the gym, he did what came most naturally to him, playing a game of half-court three-on-three, his T-shirt still gone, two dozen students along the sideline watching, some with their mouths agape.

"That was the first time I saw what was under Kobe Bryant's shirt, and for the majority of the girls in my high school, that was the first time we saw his hard, cut body," Price recalled. "There was a different side of Kobe that night that was hilarious. That wasn't him. He was prim and proper. He was never the type of guy, even with abs and everything, who would walk around without his shirt. All of a sudden, to see him let loose like that was out of the ordinary and hilarious. It just added to the fun of the night.

"He was coming out of his shell, and it was the last time I saw him."

NEXT TO his senior headshot in the 1996 edition of Enchiridion, the school's yearbook, Kobe wrote, "Thanks Mom, Dad for giving me the opportunity to go to school here in the U.S. For being there in good and bad times Sharia Shaya Ti Amo Moltissimo Matt you my main man always be.... Thanks 4a great 4 years Love you all."

He was voted the male student "Most Likely to Succeed" in the class of '96. In a candid yearbook photo, he wore a black leather jacket and wrapped his right arm around the female winner, Antje Herlyn, who became an anesthesiologist. Because he was such an overwhelming choice for that honour, his classmates did not select him as their best male athlete. That distinction went to Sean Furber, a standout on the soccer, wrestling, and lacrosse teams. After all, Kobe had played only one sport.

The main thing is getting in shape. From what I hear, it's a very long season, a lot of basketball to be played, a lot of bumping and grinding. I have to prepare myself physically so I get in shape and my legs won't get tired. A lot of rookies nowadays tend to hit a wall in the middle of the season. A lot of the great players of the past— Magic, Michael—I don't think they've ever hit that wall. I don't want to hit that wall. If I work as hard as I possibly can this summer, and I still hit the wall, then I'm going to have to work even harder.

—*KOBE BRYANT, SUMMER OF 1996*

CHAPTER 10

NOW I'M A LAKER

The two men who, more than anyone else, colluded to arrange Kobe Bryant's migration from Wynnewood to the West Coast met in the most unlikely of places: a "Mommy and Me" class. In the NBA, Arn Tellem and Jerry West were contemporaries and collaborators, with West as the Lakers' general manager and Tellem as a powerful player agent. But it wasn't until their wives had sons in the late 1980s—Karen West to Jonnie West, Nancy Tellem to Matty Tellem—and they bonded as their toddlers played with finger paint and building blocks that West and Tellem became more than just competitors on opposing sides of a negotiating table. Their family vacationed together at the Greenbrier, a luxurious resort near West's childhood home in West Virginia. Matty and Jonnie became close buddies. The trust that Tellem and West had in each other would prove crucial in the lengthy and hazardous ploy that they pulled off to get Kobe to Los Angeles and kickstart the Lakers' dynasty. Kobe was undrafted in the 1996 draft. After telling Carbone in March that he would enter the draft, he hired Joe Carbone as his full-time personal trainer, and Joe Bryant asked his friend Tony DiLeo—a fellow La Salle alumnus, a former professional player in Europe, and the Sixers' director of scouting—to tutor Kobe for his pre-draft workouts. DiLeo had Kobe perform a drill in the Fieldhouse at St. Joseph's for an hour or so each day, requiring him to shoot three hundred shots: off the dribble, on the move, and from behind the three-point arc. If Kobe missed three consecutive shots from any place, he'd have to restart the practice. "That's when I saw this inner drive he had, to be great," DiLeo recounted. "He'd miss, get frustrated, and want to try again." He was unyielding."

But what did the rest of the league think of Kobe and his potential? Tellem was unsure. The Minnesota Timberwolves' player-personnel director, Rob Babcock, compared Kobe to Kevin Garnett: "Kevin's ability as a six-eleven player was so overwhelming that it showed right away." He's a one-of-a-kind player. You don't notice that when you watch Kobe Bryant. His game does not proclaim, 'I'm a very rare skill.'" The Denver Nuggets' director of collegiate scouting, John Outlaw, stated unequivocally, "I don't think he's ready." The Sixers held the No. 1 overall pick after going 18-64 in 1995-96 and winning the draft lottery, but most of the other early-first-round picks belonged to small-market franchises, and neither Kobe nor Adidas would maximise their investment in the other if Kobe ended up in Vancouver, Indianapolis, or Cleveland. "The Lakers were the team I wanted to play for," Kobe remarked, but the Lakers were drafted 24th overall. They'd have to find a way to get a higher pick if they wanted Kobe as badly as he wanted them.

So Tellem created a strategy to capitalise on the uncertainty around Kobe. "We had to recognize," he said, "that we might have a unique opportunity." Joe Bryant reiterated to Tellem that Kobe was one of the top draft picks. Tellem organised workouts with clubs around the top of the first round to get a better feel of where Kobe may fall in the pecking order of prospects... but not all of them. Tellem may influence the process by having Kobe decline to work out for specific teams, giving them the opportunity to evaluate him in person. This would temper those teams' interest in drafting Kobe. The method is unlikely to work in today's NBA, when general managers are more likely to select the best available player, regardless of his agent's behind-the-scenes manoeuvrings. However, this was not the current NBA. It was 1996. The idea that Tellem could manipulate the process at the request of his young client infuriated him. What was this youngster thinking? Kobe only worked out for a few teams. Then Tellem called in a favour with a friend, arranging for Kobe to have a private session with West.

"I wanted to get Jerry's opinion," Tellem explained. "I told him, 'I want to do this privately.'" 'I'd want to hear what you think.'"

Two workouts followed, at the Inglewood YMCA and "on a side street somewhere," according to Kobe, that convinced West that

Kobe would be the NBA's next Greatest Player. In the first, Kobe so completely beat recently departed Lakers guard Michael Cooper—forty years old at the time, still in good shape, and one of the league's finest perimeter defenders throughout his career—that West called time on the workout after fifteen minutes. "I thought that Kobe was possibly better than the players we had on the team at the time," he writes in his autobiography West by West. "I've never seen a workout like that in my life." "I meant it when I said enough." Cooper was astonished by how physically powerful Kobe was, particularly in the low post, indicating how much Kobe's work with Carbone had aided him. In the second quarter, in front of West and Lakers coach Del Harris—Joe's coach with the Houston Rockets—Kobe dominated Dontae' Jones, a six-foot-eight small forward who had led Mississippi State to the Final Four as a senior just a few months before. In the NCAA tournament, I'm beating up on a regional MVP, he reasoned. I would have exploded if I had gone to college. I would have been murdered. Kobe called Tellem from his hotel room.

"How'd you do?" Tellem inquired, his anxiety visible to Kobe. "How'd you do?"

"I did fantastic. "Everything went swimmingly."

"OK, OK. Really? Really? Man, I adore you. "I adore you."

"Hey, Arn, take a chill pill."

The Lakers had only won one postseason series in the five years since reaching the NBA Finals in 1991, where they were defeated in five games by Michael Jordan and the Bulls. "I'm about to shake up this team this summer," West told Tellem. I'd like to have Kobe and construct my team around him and the other player I'm interested in." The "other player" was Shaquille O'Neal, who was leaving the Orlando Magic after four years. So West hatched a plan with the

Charlotte Hornets, who had the No. 13 pick: if none of the first twelve teams selected Kobe, the Hornets would draft him, then trade him to the Lakers for centre Vlade Divac. It was up to Tellem, Sonny Vaccaro, and the Bryants to make sure Kobe was still accessible when fortunate number 13 arrived. Kobe felt conflicted about the Sixers selecting him with the first choice in the draft. The prestige of becoming "the best player in the draft" sounded intriguing. But then... his patron, John Lucas, was gone. In May, the Sixers fired Lucas and hired a new general manager, Brad Greenberg, as well as a new head coach, Johnny Davis. And if Kobe was the first player chosen, he would have no team against which to hold a grudge. The number one choice is not passed up. None of the league's other teams explicitly underestimate the No. 1 pick because none of them got the opportunity to draft him. Nobody can argue with the No. 1 pick. "I want people to say, 'Awww, you messed up because you didn't take him,'" he remarked not long after the draft. "That's exactly what I want."

The Sixers, for their part, considered drafting Kobe even though they, like the rest of the league, considered Georgetown guard Allen Iverson to be the draft's top player. Both DiLeo and Gene Shue, who is now a scout for the Sixers, encouraged Greenberg to consider it, even suggesting that the Sixers trade Jerry Stackhouse to get another first-round pick, allowing them to draft Iverson and Kobe. "I knew how much they believed in him," Greenberg said, "and I do believe that if Gene or Tony had the opportunity to make the pick, they very well could have chosen Kobe." (After the Sixers went 22-60 in 1996-97, Greenberg and Davis were fired, and DiLeo, as acting director of basketball operations, approached Mitch Kupchak, the Lakers' deputy general manager, and inquired whether he and West would be amenable to dealing Kobe. He hadn't been on the phone with Kupchak for long. "They knew exactly what they had," DiLeo explained. "They didn't exactly laugh at me, but they did.") Mike Egan even called Sixers headquarters the day before the selection, informing the receptionist that he was one of Kobe Bryant's coaches and needed to talk with Greenberg. When Greenberg called him again later that afternoon, Egan was taken aback. Greenberg later stated that he had no recall of speaking with Egan, but Egan described their conversation in full.

The Washington Bullets had not had a winning season in Nash's six years as general manager, and he departed the team in the spring of 1996 in the kind of coerced departure that is frequent in professional sports and is sometimes covered up with euphemistic terminology. Nash was released by the Bullets. Soon after, the Nets hired him to work alongside and mentor Calipari, who had never worked in the NBA before, and Nash's connection with Kobe and friendship with Joe Bryant provided the Nets an advantage in the Kobe sweepstakes. He worked out for them three times, each time more amazing than the last. Willis Reed, the Nets' vice president of basketball operations and a former centre on the Knicks' great teams of the early 1970s, was six feet ten and had golf umbrella-like hands. He jiggled one of his gloves around Kobe's biceps and added, "You ain't so little." (Carbone was pleased with the compliment.) Calipari delayed the game so he could test Kobe's shooting range against former UCLA forward Ed O'Bannon, the Nets' first-round pick in 1995. Calipari urged Kobe to shoot from closer to half-court after he hit a string of three-pointers.

"Let's see if you can make something from back here," he proposed.

Kobe took five shots and made them all.

"What the hell?" exclaimed Calipari. "How did this happen?" "We assumed you couldn't shoot."

Kobe made a shaky motion with his head. Fine. Allow folks to believe I can't shoot. It's better for me.

Better for the Nets as well. Jerry West had previously called Nash and offered Divac in return for the eighth overall pick. Nash had

138

declined him. He told West that the Nets weren't ready to win right away. They intended to construct through the draft. "We zeroed in on Kobe," Nash said. "We already knew he was going to be our guy."

Calipari and Nash welcomed Joe and Pam Bryant for dinner on Tuesday, June 25, the night before the NBA draft, which was held that year at the Continental Airlines Arena in East Rutherford, New Jersey, the Nets' home arena. Calipari and Nash were both living out of a local hotel because the team had hired them so recently. They informed the Bryants that Kobe would be drafted by the Nets.

So, according to Joe, he'll start as a rookie and be an All-Star in his second season.

"After they left," Nash explained, "we both thought to ourselves, 'Typical father, high aspirations.'" It would be incredible if he could do that, but we weren't expecting it."

The following day, shortly after midday, with the draft still more than seven hours away, Kobe laid in bed in the hotel where all of the prospective draftees were staying. Tellem and Joe went over everything one last time with him.

"We can definitely have the Nets," Tellem assured him. "Are you still interested in joining the Lakers? Even though I believe I have control over the situation, there is a chance that some team will still take you. The Nets may not sign you, and you may find up somewhere you don't like as much as New Jersey."

Kobe reached up, grabbed a piece of Tellem's shirt, and drew him closer.

"That's why I hired you," he explained. "You'll get it done."

Meanwhile, Calipari and Nash were having lunch with Joe Taub, the Nets' ownership group's point man, to brief him on their selection strategy. Taub was disappointed that the team chose Kobe, or any high school player, over Syracuse forward John Wallace. Furthermore, Taub told Nash that the Nets would be wasting time and money on Kobe. The team had only two winning seasons in eleven years and resided in the shadow of the New York region's other, historically superior NBA franchise, so Taub assumed Kobe would leave at the first opportunity. "Because of the Knicks," Nash remembered, "the Nets had a terrible second-class mentality." "They thought they'd never be able to catch the Knicks."

Around 2:00 p.m., Calipari and Nash had just returned to the office when Kobe contacted Calipari and Tellem called Nash. Both conveyed the same message: while Kobe appreciated the Nets' interest in him, he refused to play for them. In fact, if they did draft him, he'd rather go back to Europe and sign with a team there than end up in the swamps of New Jersey.

Tellem assumed Nash would draft Kobe if given the opportunity, but Calipari was a soft target, a young coach eager to please his bosses, conscious of the culture he hoped to instil in his new team, and eager to avoid having to manage a relationship with a player who had already stated his desire not to play for the Nets. Nash worked the phones and learned of the Lakers-Hornets deal, but Tellem received assistance from an unexpected source: his main opponent, agent David Falk. Falk represented Kerry Kittles and had been lobbying the Nets to select him at No. 8 in the draft. "We liked Kerry Kittles a lot," Nash said, "but he would have been our backup." So Falk phoned Calipari and told him that if we didn't sign Kittles, we wouldn't be able to sign one of his free agents."

Falk's warning was dismissed by Nash as an agent's ruse, but for Calipari, the pressure to not sign Kobe was now double-barreled. The two guys passed Tellem, Falk, and Vaccaro, who were huddled together, as they walked through the arena's tunnels toward the Nets' locker room, where the team's front-office executives were having supper at six o'clock. "What are you going to do?" one of the three said.

"You'll know when we make the pick," Nash replied.

Nash, on the other hand, had no idea. Moving on to the locker room, Nash attempted to persuade Calipari to call all of these bluffs, adhere to their original plan, and choose Kobe. Don't worry, John Nash said. You have a five-year contract. Even if we miss this pick, it's a freebie. You're not going to get fired because of this draft. He didn't know what Calipari's choice would be until after the dinner started, when Calipari stood up and told the folks there that if Kerry Kittles was available at No. 8, the Nets would take him. If he wasn't, they'd go for Kobe Bryant.

"The wind went out of my sails," Nash recounted.

Would Kobe have truly turned down the Nets to play in Europe? "I'm not going to answer that," Tellem declared in 2020. "That question will always be unanswered." Such a step would not have been unusual. Only seven years before, Duke's Danny Ferry, the No. 2 overall pick in the 1989 draft, had signed with an Italian team rather than report to the hapless Los Angeles Clippers. However, Ferry did not have the same marketing and endorsement riches at stake as Kobe.

"Kobe's not going to turn down being the eighth pick in the draft to play in Europe," Vaccaro added. "Use your common sense. What the hell are you terrified of if you felt taking him was the greatest option? Why are you being compensated? He's going to Italy rather than finishing ninth in the N-B-fucking-A? Are you insane? I didn't need him in the hell of Italy. This is what happens when history is built on deception. It is self-sustaining. The greater you are as a business, an individual, or a mythological talent, the bigger the deception. What the fuck is going on? Kerry Kittles was an excellent player. He was an excellent professional. However, do not use Kobe as a foil because you 'thought he was going somewhere.' What you did was form an expert opinion."

Thick, dark drapes draped from high poles along the arena floor created a green room where the players, dressed in boxy, too-big suits, sat with their families and agents at tables beside a buffet. Nobody ate. There are too many nerves. Joe and Pam, Sharia and Shaya, Chubby and John Cox, Sonny and Pam Vaccaro, and Tellem sat with Kobe. Gregg Downer and Mike Egan were in the stands, peering down at NBA commissioner David Stern every time he announced a pick. Stern could be heard through the drapes, but he could only see him on a nearby television. Joe and Pam twitched. Each of them squeezed Kobe's hand.

Iverson is headed to the Sixers...

Marcus Camby is headed to the Toronto Raptors...

Shareef Abdur-Rahim has been assigned to the Vancouver Grizzlies...

It doesn't matter if I'm the fourth pick or if I go to New Jersey, Sacramento, or elsewhere. I speak the truth.

Antoine Walker, No. 6 to the Boston Celtics...

Lorenzen Wright was selected seventh overall by the Clippers...

If Coach Calipari chooses me, I'll be a fantastic player.

Kerry Kittles joins the Nets...

Here I come, Los Angeles...

Todd Fuller, No. 11 overall, to the Golden State Warriors...

Vitaly Potapenko was selected 12th overall by the Cleveland Cavaliers...

Don't trip, Kobe. Take care not to trip.

Downer and Egan were overjoyed when Stern announced that the Hornets had chosen Kobe. They could road-trip to some of Kobe's games because Charlotte was a short flight or a doable drive away. Joe had to take a twenty-minute break from the post-pick interviews and afterglow to find them.

"Kobe," he said, "is going to be a Laker."

And it appeared that he wouldn't be. Divac stated that he would retire rather than join the Hornets. Bob Bass, Charlotte's general manager, called West to withdraw from the transaction. "Bob, we have a deal, goddamn it," West declared. "Vlade is not going away." "Believe me." Tellem summoned Bass and unleashed a torrent of rage that Tellem's secretary, Elissa Fisher Grabow, would recall for years: screaming, stomping his feet, his neck veins popping, his mouth spewing spittle, "so much physical chaos," Grabow recounted, to compel Bass to finalise the exchange. When Divac's wife persuaded him not to resign, the teams agreed to meet on July 1.The repercussions for Kobe and Tellem were quick and severe. The first was a seventeen-year-old prima donna dictating terms to the whole NBA, and the second was the enabler of a summer-long plot to compel his client to a favourable destination. According to Jerry

Reynolds, the Sacramento Kings' player-personnel director, "it's depressing that any player and his representation, who have their choice of entering or electing not to enter the draft, turn around and don't follow the rules of the draft." According to Timothy Dwyer of The Philadelphia Inquirer, Kobe "didn't help himself or his image." With his teenage power play, he turned off a lot of sneaker-buying admirers." The stress of obtaining Kobe and signing O'Neal in mid-July sent West into a condition of weariness and melancholy that landed him in the hospital for three days. Kobe, on the other hand, had obtained what he wanted and felt neither guilty nor exhausted by the process.

"Now I'm a Laker," he announced later that summer. "At first, I was astonished and shocked. Now it's just, "I want to win a championship." I'm not going in there and thinking, "I want to have a good rookie season, and if we win the championship, fine." Fine if we make it to the Western Conference finals.' That is not the case. I'd like to win a title. I need to go there right away. It's going to be like that every year. If I win a championship next year, the next year I'm going to come back saying, 'Look, dude, I want to get a championship again. Man, Shaq, come on. Let's get started. Let's go grab another. Michael received four. Let's go for five. Let's go for five.' That's how things will be from now on."

Independence Day, a nighttime concert by Patti LaBelle and the Philadelphia Orchestra, a fireworks display on the Benjamin Franklin Parkway outside the Philadelphia Museum of Art, a zephyr cleansing the evening, leaving it refreshing and cool after a recent rain. It's been eight days since the NBA draft and three days since the deal was finalised. Kobe was out with his cousin Sharif Butler, and he was wearing a baseball cap that was pulled low on his head so no one would know him. He was recognized by someone. He despised it. It was all so foolish, what people said to him, how they acted around him, how confident they felt. He'd gone to a ten-dollar cover party in West Philadelphia the previous weekend. He was standing at the door when a female he didn't know approached him and asked for ten dollars to get into the party. Lend? Don't be concerned, she said. I'll repay you. I'll send the money to the Lakers. I know you're wealthy. Could you trust this nonsense? Was he some sort of national bank? He apologised to her. I only have plastic. I've got you covered if they accept Visa or Mastercard. If not, what do you intend to do? Can you cut the plastic in half? Her entire social posture irritated him, as if he was obliged to give her the money, as if she had the right to ask him for it, even though he had no idea who the heck she was.

"I don't trust anybody," he later admitted.

Trust? Forget about it. Trust had vanished. Trust had died. Take a look at the parkway on the Fourth of July. A person should be intelligent enough to approach him and whisper... What about Kobe Bryant? Are you not Kobe Bryant? That was astute. That was thoughtful. But, with hundreds of people surrounding him, one man had to turn and half-yell, Kobe Bryant?! And now his secret had been revealed, and there were so many people seeking, begging, and pressing on his autograph... Please sign this for me... Kobe, come on... Man, I saw you defeat Chester... and you had no idea who or what might attack you at any moment. There is no security. There will be no patting down. That is not the case. Guy could become envious and start saying things. Guy might have a gun...

"Man," he said to Butler, "I'm feeling uneasy." This is the last time I'll leave the house without a bodyguard."

They stayed for another ten minutes, for a total of a half hour, watched the fireworks, and then went. People had previously recognized him. His face was well-known. But he had seen something in just a short time: they were reacting differently to him, expecting something from him, making demands of him, absolute strangers with their hands out. And he hadn't reacted to them like this before, like if they were all hazards in waiting, as if any of them could be brandishing something dreadful in those hands. This was his new life.

On July 27, 1996, Kobe and his pals Kevin Sanchez and Anthony Bannister met Charlie Mack, a bodyguard and promoter for actor/rapper Will Smith, at the Jewish Community Center in Wynnewood, the three of them still united by their love of rap. Kobe, Sanchez, and Bannister had established CHEIZAW, an abbreviation for a long name: Canon Homo sapiens Eclectic Iconic Zaibatsu Abstract Words. Mack had met Kobe and Joe Bryant through the Bryants' music industry contacts, and he had consented to listen to some of the group's tracks. CHEIZAW rhymed for Mack for three to four hours, with Sanchez and Bannister taking a fifteen-minute break to rush to McDonald's for some food. Around 6:00 p.m., Kobe left. The audition resulted in a recording contract for CHEIZAW a few months later, but Kobe's rap career lasted only four years. In the year 2000, Sony dropped him.

On that afternoon, a man with his face hidden under a Stroehmann bread bag robbed a 7-Eleven on City Avenue. A witness chose a photo of Sanchez, who had a youth police record, from a group of eight. Sanchez weighed 185 pounds and was six feet tall. The suspect was characterised as 5'8" and 120 pounds by the witness. Despite this, Sanchez was convicted of armed robbery after a two-day trial in September 1998, spending more than five years in prison before his release in 2007. "It isn't Kobe's fault that I went to jail," he once claimed. He had figured he couldn't lose at trial, so he hadn't insisted on Kobe testifying as an alibi witness on his behalf. So Kobe never testified, and his friend excused him from his absence. This was now his life as well. In the summer of 1996, weeks passed. Kobe was in Los Angeles, at UCLA's gym, stretching on the court before a pickup run. Someone he hadn't met yet walked in the door. That's Magic, man. Magic Johnson was 37 years old and had just played 32 games for the Lakers in the 1995-96 season, the final 32 games of his career. He wasn't from a bygone era. He wasn't even Michael Cooper, who had been out of the league for six years.

"Hey, how you doin', young fella?"

"I'm doing well," Kobe stated.

Kobe saw his outfit right away: shorts, a tank top, and sneakers.

I'll be pitted against Magic. Cool.

For the first few games, they were on the same squad, freelancing and playing off one other. They then separated. Three games were won by Kobe's side. Magic, not pleased, returned the next day and won three himself, their banter flying like corn in a popper.

"I remember one time we had a pick-and-roll, and we forced him to switch out, so I had the wing," Kobe remarked later. So I'm alone with Magic. I'm looking, but I'm not really paying attention. 'Hold up,' I say. I have Magic on me. 'I'm taking him to the hoop.' So, bang, I go to the basket, go up for a layup on one side, and he fouls me. Another man moves up from the baseline, so I hang and go to the other side, scoop it, lay it off the glass, and get a and-one. 'Yeah, man, OK, OK, OK, excellent move.'"

There is no crowd. There is no applause. There is no state championship on the line. Just Magic, the man with the world's most renowned smile, with an implicit and unstated inquiry, the one that matters most on every basketball court: What have you got? There is no envy. There is no resentment. There was no whining about Kobe shooting too much or holding back a lesser player. Just Magic, cementing his place. Yes, sir. That's a smart move. This was now his life as well.

It's always been my dream and goal to play professional basketball. I've always loved the game. I love the smell of the leather, the hardwood, the concrete of the playground, the swish of the net. I just really love the game. I don't know where that came from. It's always been there.

—KOBE BRYANT

CHAPTER 11

OPEN GYM

Elissa Fisher lives in a Marina del Rey townhouse across the street from Jerry's Famous Deli. Grabow pondered what she would say to Kobe Bryant if he contacted her, since she knew he would ultimately call her while he hit one air ball... two air balls... three... four?... at the Delta Center in Salt Lake City. Grabow, as Arn Tellem's assistant, played an important role in Kobe's rookie season with the Lakers: she was the non-basketball person in his life who was there to help him make the transition from high school to the NBA. She didn't follow the sport and wouldn't watch a game unless one of Tellem's clients was involved, but this one was on TV: Game five of the Western Conference semifinals, Utah Jazz leading the Lakers by three games to one, Kobe taking the potential game-winning jumper at the end of regulation and missing... Nothing, three more shots in overtime that missed... Nothing, his legs wet pasta, after eighty games in the NBA, the Lakers' season ending with a 98-93 loss. Grabow may have been termed a fixer, but that term didn't exactly convey everything she did for Kobe. He referred to her as "E," always "E"; a former preschool teacher only eleven years his senior, Grabow believed she was of Kobe's generation, or at least near enough to be able to interact with him better than Tellem could. She didn't need him for anything. She was merely there to assist him, and she believed he would require her assistance now. He'd be devastated, I'm sure. How am I supposed to perk up his spirits?

Finally, the phone call. Kobe hadn't bothered to wait until the Lakers' team plane had landed in L.A. When he called her, it was still in the air.

"Have Palisades' gym open for me," he said. "I want to go shoot."

Palisades High School was only around three miles away from Kobe's house. Grabow's understanding of Kobe's brief directive was unmistakable. She was supposed to wake up everyone she needed to wake up, phone whoever she needed to call, and do whatever she needed to do to get him into the school's basketball gym that night. He was not upset. There was no quaver in his voice, no sign that his performance had embarrassed him. On a Monday night in May, it was well after 10:00 p.m., West Coast time. The next morning would be school.

"Make sure it's open," Kobe instructed.

Maybe he was expecting that terrible night. Perhaps the embarrassment of those air balls was karma for a conversation he had with Tellem the summer before his rookie year, for eleven months of juggling all the contradictory qualities that would make him an incredible basketball player and, at the time, made it reasonable to wonder if he was setting himself up for an Icarus moment. Kobe and Tellem would argue about everything—sports, politics, music, history—and one day, Tellem asked him what he felt about facing Jazz point guard John Stockton.

"Well," Kobe explained, "I grew up playing against all of these Catholic League players." I've played with a lot of players like that."

Tellem was stunned. He knew right once who Kobe was referring to: men who scratch and claw and play aggressive, often filthy defence, guys who are short, scrappy, and white. "This is fucking John Stockton," he pointed out to Kobe. You may recall John Stockton, a member of the United States' "Dream Team" at the 1992 Summer Olympics in Barcelona. John Stockton, who had led the NBA in assists for the previous nine seasons, went on to play in 10 All-Star Games and set the league's career assists and steals records, was elected into the Naismith Memorial Hall of Fame. John Stockton, who Kobe had reduced to a cultural caricature.

"No problem," Kobe responded. "I know who John Stockton is."

An ESPN reporter had asked him if he had any games marked on his calendar. And Kobe had answered, "Of course not," which was... well, not true. "You know damn well I'm looking forward to Charlotte," he'd later added. "I'm looking forward to the 76ers on November 26." I have a bounty on Stackhouse." He was still waging his father's conflicts, as he had learned in Italy, and as Anthony Gilbert had witnessed and heard from him on those playground courts. "I heard from Joe that he was ahead of his time. "He was never given a fair shake," Tellem remarked. "From childhood, a son absorbs and picks up on these things, and this was a very close family." Kobe took it all in and used it to shape who he was." Grabow saw Kobe's arrogance as a ruse, a device that an ambitious adolescent depended on to get him where he wanted to go. What else could it be to her? After finalising his Adidas contract and the three-year, $3.65 million contract he signed with the Lakers, Kobe had welcomed Grabow there with Joe, Pam, and Shaya, all of whom had moved in with him, as well as Sonny and Pam Vaccaro, who lived a few houses away. Kobe's house was breathtaking: an all-white exterior; an ocean view; white marble floors inside; a winding staircase; couches with massive, inviting pillows; ever-present aromas of vanilla sugar, cookies warming in the oven, Pam's homemade fried chicken and macaroni-and-cheese that her baby loved so much; a mother and a family sheltering him, taking care of him, feeding his soul.

"It's really simple to me," Kobe remarked before his debut with the Lakers. "I was born and raised in Italy." I had just my sisters, mother, and father on whom I could trust. We had such a close relationship, such a wonderful friendship as a result of it, and when we returned here, we put it to use. When I see my classmates arguing with their brothers and sisters and saying 'I hate her' or 'I don't like him' or whatever, I just want to get home and see my mother, see my father, and enjoy the family atmosphere that I have, because I know it won't last forever."That's why my mother and father need to come out there and live with me so I can enjoy their company. Then, when the bird is ready to leave the nest, that is the time. But I'm going to appreciate them while I can because you never know what can happen."

Gregg Downer and Jeremy Treatman flew out to Los Angeles for a visit that coincided with the start of the Lakers' regular season, and they arrived to Sharia and Shaya sitting on Kobe's bed and eating popcorn during a family movie night on a Friday, to Kobe's aeroplane hangar-size closet filled with Lakers jerseys and Adidas gear, as well as designer clothes—Tommy Hilfiger, Perry Ellis, Guess, Polo—that companies had sent to him. It was so strange, Kobe said to Treatman. He assumed he'd have enough money to buy whatever shirts and sneakers he wanted, but it turned out that wealthy people didn't have to buy anything because everyone wanted them to endorse their clothes and products. So the firms hiked their prices on the poor while giving him the goods for free. That caught me off guard.

"There was an innocence about what was going on," said Downer. "He was naive, but there was tenderness."

The area around his bed was empty except for two items: a VHS tape of Lower Merion's season-in-review, a highlight montage that Treatman had produced and set to the song "One Shining Moment," the soundtrack of CBS's coverage of the NCAA men's basketball tournament, and his state-championship medal, which was dangling from one of the bedposts.

"Where is everything else?" Treatman inquired.

"I don't think I need anything else!" Kobe stated. "This is all I need until I start accomplishing things in the NBA."

It was wonderful, perhaps too perfect, as if Kobe had purposefully left out those souvenirs for Downer and Treatman. They said no.

Kobe would never do something like that. Kobe adored Lower Merion.

The arrogance wasn't a ruse, as Grabow thought at the time. Innocence and arrogance may coexist within Kobe, manifesting themselves in different contexts and ways. He broke his wrist three weeks before training camp during a pickup game in Venice Beach. "It wasn't going to stop me from doing my thing," he declared. Del Harris, on the other hand, did. Kobe's wrist healed in time for him to play in a couple of preseason games, but after making a flashy move and missing a pull-up jump shot, he came to the sideline only to have Harris admonish him: That kind of thing might have worked in high school, but it wouldn't work in the NBA. Awww, shit, thought Kobe. It's going to be a long motherfucking season. And it would be from his point of view. Harris's coaching of Joe in Houston years before earned Kobe no special treatment, and Kobe showed him no kindness in return.

What was Harris thinking by benching Kobe for two games in late November, having him play less than ten minutes in his first game versus Michael and the Bulls at the United Center in December, and then having him play just three minutes more in the teams' rematch in February? Sure, the Lakers would win 56 games. Sure, Shaquille O'Neal would take Kobe under his wing, inviting him over for home-cooked meals, and Kobe would declare, "Shaq's like my older brother." We've been inseparable since the beginning." Sure, Kobe would put up 31 points in the NBA Rookie Game. But he would think about what he didn't do or what Harris wouldn't let him do. Regardless, Kobe would play 71 games in the regular season, averaging 15.5 minutes and 7.6 points per game, a massive workload for an eighteen-year-old rookie. Regardless of Harris' failure to rein in Kobe's offensive inclinations, Kobe would average 13.8 shots per 36 minutes, the second-highest rate on the team, ahead of starting guards Eddie Jones and Nick Van Exel, and trailing only O'Neal. Regardless, Kobe scored twelve points in his debut game in Philadelphia, a victory over the Sixers, while his Lower Merion coaches and friends cheered him on. It didn't matter that Harris trusted him enough to play him more than twenty-eight minutes in Game Five against the Jazz, or that with the game tied late in the fourth quarter, he would gather the Lakers in the huddle and call a play for Kobe. Allow the child to bring the ball up. Allow him to go one-on-one with Utah's greatest defender, Bryon Russell. Allow the NBA's youngest player to decide the fate of one of the league's most decorated franchises in the postseason. Kobe just saw shackles. All Kobe saw was Allen Iverson playing forty minutes per night for the Sixers and scoring twenty-three to twenty-four points per night, Kerry Kittles playing thirty-six minutes per night for John Calipari and the Nets, and a coach in Los Angeles who was holding him back and burying him on the bench out of spite.

"You're against the whole thing I'm doing, coming into the league in the first place," he explained after the season in response to Harris' coaching. "He's just looking for anything to bring me down for the entire season." It's amusing because people either don't want to see what's going on or are unaware of what's going on. But I believe it is hard to ignore what is going on. 'Go in there and do your thing,' Shaq had encouraged me a couple of times. Play your own game. Allow the game to come to you, but go out and do your thing. If he drags you out, he drags you out. He's going to drag you out anyway.' He's always seeking an opportunity to sit me down and irritate me. But it doesn't matter to me. He's a jerk."

He was lonely—how could he not be?—hungry for freedom but unfamiliar with it. His teammates were all male. He wasn't quite one yet. As the season progressed, he began to phone Grabow instead of driving back to Pacific Palisades immediately after games. I'd want to come over. He didn't want to return home, but he didn't have any other options. She was 29, just like another big sister. She'd bake him brownies, and they'd spend hours watching episodes of Mr. Bean, the British sitcom, on HBO. "He was obsessed with Mr. Bean," said Grabow. But every now and again, she'd be holding a dinner party or her roommate would have people around, and he'd drop by. He'd sit on Grabow's couch in a room separate from everyone else, the TV on, not even safe enough to introduce himself, everything awkward,

until the reactions of those partygoers shifted from He's a Laker!
Why is this person stopping by again?

"It wasn't like he'd entered my friend's world," Grabow later
explained. "Kobe lacked social skills; he was uncomfortable just
talking to strangers." But he believed in me, and he believed in very
few others. So it was a case of 'OK, the babysitting continues.'"He
enjoyed being looked after. But I noticed a natural change of 'I don't
want to be with my parents anymore. That is something I no longer
desire. 'I want to be an adult.' He was determined to prove everyone
wrong because everyone said, 'He's a bust.' 'I'm going to accomplish
this,' it seemed like tunnel vision.

Except that tunnel vision had led to that agonising stretch against the
Jazz, a fourteen-footer and three three-pointers in five minutes, all
wide open, none close... What was the appropriate parallel? Perhaps
a singer forgetting the words to the national anthem, or the
Hindenburg collapsing, a choking or collapse or disaster so naked
and public that, if you were witnessing it, you would feel forced to
reach out and aid the poor youngster... No, I don't need you, this kid
would say. I'm perfectly fine. You're a jerk. I can handle it myself.
Check to see if the gym is open.

Grabow got off the phone. Kobe was having a problem. She was
going to mend it. She contacted the officials and coaches at Palisades
High School. They'd drive to the school in the middle of the night,
open the doors, and give Kobe as much time as he wanted. Once
there, he would stay all night, watch the sun rise, and then have Joe
Carbone put him through another three days of exercises, drills, and
lifts until his legs and jumper returned to him, and he could begin his
off-season. First, the Lakers' plane had to safely land. At 2:00 a.m., it
did. He drove straight to Palisades High from the airport, never
stopping at home. Of course, he hadn't and couldn't read the
newspapers yet. He couldn't read the upcoming New York Times
article that would describe his four air balls as "a scene straight out
of Ripley's." Or the San Bernardino journalist, who would be

perplexed: "How come the ball is in his hands for the final shot with the score tied in regulation?" The Lakers treated Kobe as if he were Michael Jordan in the final game of the season." He may have overheard Van Exel tell the Los Angeles Times in the locker room, "He's going to be a great player in this league, but maybe the season caught up with him a little on those threes." He fell a bit short." It would be a few days, though, before Rockets forward Matt Bullard stated, "By the time I was eighteen, I had not shot four air balls in my life." I believe it fosters... the idea of young kids coming up not being able to make shots. They don't practise their shots. They concentrate on their open-court game, as well as breaking down opponents off the dribble and dunking." He'd swallow it all, telling everyone that none of the criticism hurt him, yet in reality, every nagging fear, every reservation about his future invaded his being like a germ and burned in his brain like a fever. Chester. Utah. The first draft. Del Harris is an actor. Everything would be read by him. He had always done so.

He entered the parking lot. On his bedpost was a state championship medal. Purple and gold dominate his wardrobe. There had been no change. Everything was in flux. He was eighteen years old and alone in a high school gymnasium, wearing sneakers and holding a basketball. The rest of the world felt he was a failure. That was all OK. That was perfect. Most others did not perceive him in the same light that he perceived himself. They couldn't see what he had done, and what he was still willing to do, to transform his dreams and compulsions into something permanent, into the existential mortar and stone of an unforgettable life. They didn't know the whole tale, not yet. A baby with the name of a restaurant. A child who had brought a community together. A teen whose youth was only now receding into the distance and darkness of his recollection. They'd figure it out. He would see to it that they learned. He had plenty of time. He had so much time on his hands.

The first shot slipped between his fingers.

The contents of this book may not be copied, reproduced or transmitted without the express written permission of the author or publisher. Under no circumstances will the publisher or author be responsible or liable for any damages, compensation or monetary loss arising from the information contained in this book, whether directly or indirectly. .

Disclaimer Notice:

Although the author and publisher have made every effort to ensure the accuracy and completeness of the content, they do not, however, make any representations or warranties as to the accuracy, completeness, or reliability of the content. , suitability or availability of the information, products, services or related graphics contained in the book for any purpose. Readers are solely responsible for their use of the information contained in this book

Every effort has been made to make this book possible. If any omission or error has occurred unintentionally, the author and publisher will be happy to acknowledge it in upcoming versions.